DISCIPLE FAST TRACK

CONTENTS

AS YOU LEAD DISCIPLE FAST TRACK

A Long History

Since 1987, DISCIPLE Bible study has reached millions of people worldwide, introducing the grand sweep of Scripture in a thirty-four-week format. Now DISCIPLE FAST TRACK maintains the integrity and principles of the original study, but its modifications can better meet the needs of a hectic world. Participants still receive a thorough introduction to the Bible but in almost a third less time. FAST TRACK is not a replacement for the original; it is simply a practical option.

Susan Wilke Fuquay, the developer and general editor of DISCIPLE FAST TRACK, is a United Methodist Christian educator who has worked at St. Luke's United Methodist Church in Indianapolis, Indiana. For more than twenty-five years, Susan has been directly involved with DISCIPLE Bible study. She coedited the youth version of DISCIPLE, was a DISCIPLE trainer at national training events, and has personally facilitated more than thirty DISCIPLE groups. Susan beta tested the FAST TRACK study with nine hundred churches and personally led more than two hundred people through the FAST TRACK model.

How It Works

The course uses much of the same content from the original DISCIPLE Study Manual, but the class time and course length have been adjusted for busy lifestyles. Short videos (5–7 minutes) introduce each session, setting the stage for your weekly group meetings.

Features

Group Meetings

DISCIPLE FAST TRACK participants meet for a total of twenty-four weeks. There are twelve sessions in the Old Testament and twelve in the New Testament. Groups typically start the Old Testament in early fall and finish before Thanksgiving; they then start the New Testament in January and finish around Easter.

Each group session lasts approximately seventy-five minutes—half the time of traditional DISCIPLE classes. Churches are able to fit classes in on Sunday mornings, lunch hours, during evening children's programming, and even early in the morning before the workday begins. Traditional small groups that meet in homes easily cover the material within their normal time frames.

FAST TRACK is designed for small groups of 8–16, as traditional DISCIPLE is intended. But unlike the traditional version, FAST TRACK easily adapts for groups of 17–100. Large groups simply need table leaders who will lead the small group discussions around the tables with provided discussion sheets or other discussion-focused activities during each class session. Many churches have used the large group model to allow the pastor to lead large numbers of people while maintaining the intimacy of the small group.

Leader Guide and Study Manuals

This Leader Guide skillfully directs FAST TRACK leaders through the biblical narrative in each of the twenty-four sessions. All handouts are provided. The DISCIPLE FAST TRACK Old Testament and New Testament Study Manuals, each consisting of twelve sessions, are used together for this twenty-four-week study.

DVD

Each week's group meeting begins with a video from the DISCIPLE FAST TRACK DVD. The DVD includes an introduction, promotional clip, and twenty-four short videos (5–7 minutes), one for each session. Each video begins with a two-minute, illustrated review of the previous week's lesson. The review recalls the key word, the "Marks of Discipleship," and main biblical stories and passages that you discussed. Following the review, the host introduces the lesson for the current week. The video is designed to help you think about key theological issues and to set the stage for your group conversation.

Justin Coleman, your host for the Old Testament videos, is Chief Ministry Officer of The United Methodist Publishing House in Nashville, Tennessee. Justin combines skills as a pastor, teacher, social innovator, developer of leaders, and team builder. Before coming to Nashville, he was lead pastor of the Gethsemane Campus of St. Luke's United Methodist Church, Houston, Texas.

Jessica LaGrone, your host for the New Testament videos, is Dean of the Chapel at Asbury Theological Seminary. Jessica is an acclaimed pastor, teacher, author, and speaker who enjoys leading retreats and events at churches throughout the United States. She is the author of *Namesake: When God Rewrites Your Story*, *Broken and Blessed: How God Changed the World Through One Imperfect Family*, and *Set Apart: Holy Habits of Prophets and Kings*.

More information and helpful handouts for DISCIPLE FAST TRACK are available at *adultbiblestudies.com/fasttrack*.

DISCIPLE

FAST TRACK

OLD TESTAMENT

1   THE CREATING GOD

PREPARE FOR THE SESSION

Prepare and make enough copies of a group roster (include names and contact information) to hand out to each participant at the beginning of this session. Make enough copies of the Small Group Discussion Guide (found on page 9) to distribute to groups of 4–6 participants in your class.

WELCOME AND INTRODUCTION (15 MINUTES TOTAL)

Offer a personal welcome.

Hand out the copies of the group roster.

Ask participants to share their names and explain briefly what they hope to gain from participating in this study. (5 MINUTES)

Ask how the group did with the daily Bible reading and whether anyone needs clarification on how to use the Study Manual or how to look up Scriptures in their study Bible. Clarify as needed.

Ask participants to open their Study Manuals to Session 1. Direct the group to read aloud together the following:

Theme Word: Creation

Theme Verse: "God created humanity in God's own image, in the divine image God created them, male and female God created them" (Genesis 1:27).

Title: The Creating God

Our Human Condition:

I wonder who made me and my world. If there is a creator, what is this creator like? Why was I made? Scientists say some rocks are billions of years old and stars millions of light years away. In a universe so big, surely I am only a speck of dust. Does God really have anything to do with me? Does the Bible have any answers or power to offer me?

Ask participants to underline the parts of the human condition they most easily relate to.

Opening Prayer: Pray the prayer aloud together from this session in the Study Manual:

"Your hands have made me and set me in place.
  Help me understand so I can learn your commandments"
                    (Psalm 119:73).

VIEW THE DVD (5 MINUTES)

EXPLORE "THE CREATING GOD" (25 MINUTES)

Share the Following:

The Bible is made up of sixty-six books with a variety of types of literature in it. This week you will read samples of them. We are not yet concerned about the meaning of these verses. We just wanted you to sample a variety of literature.

1   THE CREATING GOD

Let's have a quick show of hands: Who enjoyed history the most? law? prophecy? letters? Gospels? As you observed, each type of literature has its own characteristics. Some types are easier to read than others. We will read a large portion of each type of literature!

Many different people wrote the Bible over hundreds of years. The process used to determine which writings would be in the Bible was called "the canonization of Scripture." This happened over a long period of time when authorities in the early church gathered to use specific criteria to decide which books to include and which to leave out. The collection of writings in our Bible today was finalized in A.D. 397.

We know the Bible is widely considered to be the best-selling book of all time, and it has been a major influence on literature and history, especially in Western civilization. Yet in our world today we may be skeptical of giving anything or anyone power and authority over us. We are exposed to people who often use the Bible in unappealing ways. So, how are we to read the Bible? How can we open up our minds and hearts to the impact the Bible can have on us? Let's consider the following:

Have the group turn to page 8 of the Study Manual and follow along as you read this paragraph aloud:

"When we speak of Scripture as being inspired, we are recognizing that the Scriptures were written by particular persons in particular circumstances. We are saying that the Scriptures are connected to God and, because of that connection, the Scriptures have power to bring about an encounter between God and the one who reads Scripture. The authority of Scripture, then, lies in its ability to cause encounter."

How do you understand the idea that the people who wrote the Scriptures were "inspired by God"? (Briefly discuss.)

If the Scriptures are inspired by God, then they are connected to God. Therefore, when we read the Scriptures, we can connect to God or—in other words—have encounters with God. So, let's first think about what it means to encounter God. Can some of you share with the group any examples of times you have "encountered God"? (Participants may share all types of examples, such as experiencing comfort, direction, confirmation, or healing.)

One of many ways people encounter God is when reading the Scriptures. Have any of you had an encounter with God through Scripture you can share with the group?

If you have had these encounters, how have you responded? Did you give an encounter authority in your life? For example, while reading Scripture, if you sensed you should do something, did you do it?

In the paragraph from the Study Manual, it says, "The authority of Scripture, then, lies in its ability to cause encounter." What do you think that means?

1 THE CREATING GOD

As we begin this commitment to DISCIPLE FAST TRACK, which involves daily Scripture reading, what would it mean to place yourself under the power and authority of Scripture during this class? (Briefly discuss.)

Consider Creation

Now let's begin at the very beginning of the Bible, with Creation.

In this session we read the two Creation stories in Genesis. You may find it interesting to know that there are many more ancient creation stories. Some include the sequence of days, darkness before light, and a division of the waters, but many also feature conflict between several gods. However, there is only one God, and God is the Creator. The one God, Yahweh, brought creation out of chaos by using words alone. These ideas are unique to Genesis.

ENCOURAGE SMALL GROUP DISCUSSION (15 MINUTES)

Divide the class into groups of 4–6. Hand out the Small Group Discussion Guide and ask the groups to spend the next fifteen minutes on this activity. (The leader participates in one of the small group discussions. There is no need to have groups report their discussions to the entire class or for the leader to "check up on" discussions.)

CONSIDER THE MARKS OF DISCIPLESHIP (10 MINUTES)

Disciples know they belong to God, that God has claim on them. They place themselves under the power and authority of Scripture.

Remind the group that the "Marks of Discipleship" emphasize characteristics or practices of a Christ-follower. The "mark" is the disciple's response to "Our Human Condition" found at the beginning of each session.

Have the group turn back to "Our Human Condition" in the Study Manual and read it aloud together. Then have the group turn to the "Mark of Disciple-ship" printed in italics and read it aloud together.

Divide the group into pairs to discuss the questions in the "Marks of Disciple-ship" section of the Study Manual. Suggest pairs choose the ones most interesting to them and discuss as many as time allows.

CLOSE WITH PRAYER (5 MINUTES)

Direct participants to use the space provided for prayer concerns in Session 2 and write a personal prayer in response to this week's session, such as "Help me to understand fully that I am made in the image of God," or "Help me to take better care of the earth," or "Show me how to honor the Sabbath," or "Help me to grow in my understanding of the Scriptures."

Remind participants to use the group roster and pray for each person in the coming week.

Close the group session in prayer.

1 THE CREATING GOD

SMALL GROUP DISCUSSION GUIDE
(15 MINUTES)

Ask one person to be a timekeeper and plan about 7–8 minutes per story for the discussion. As you discuss the following, refer to your Bible, the Study Manual, and any study notes to help answer the questions. Complete as much as your group can in fifteen minutes.

Silently review Genesis 1:1–2:3. Then discuss the following:

1. What does this story teach us about God?

2. What does this story teach us about humankind?

3. What does this story teach about the relationship between God and humankind?

4. Read Genesis 1:26 aloud. What do you think humankind's role is to be in the Creation?

5. Read Genesis 1:27 aloud. Share your responses to the question in your Study Manual that says, "We are made 'in God's own image.' What do you suppose that means?"

6. Read Genesis 2:2-3 aloud. Read the study notes in your Bible for these two verses. Share with one another your understanding of the Sabbath.

Silently review the second Creation story in Genesis 2:4-25. Then discuss the following questions:

1. What does this story teach us about God?

2. What does this story teach us about humankind?

3. What does this story teach about the relationship between God and humankind?

4. Open your Study Manuals to page 12 and share your answers to the first two questions: "What do you think is the meaning of God's forming 'the human from the topsoil of the fertile land?'" and "What do you think the Scripture means by continuing, 'and blew life's breath into his nostrils. The human came to life'?"

2 THE REBEL PEOPLE

PREPARE FOR THE SESSION

Make enough copies of the Small Group Discussion Guide (found on page 13) to distribute to groups of 4–6 participants in your class.

WELCOME AND INTRODUCTION (5 MINUTES)

Greet participants and ask: How did you do with your daily reading this week?
Ask participants to open their Study Manuals to Session 2. Direct the group to read aloud together the following:

Theme Word: Sin

Theme Verse:
"Because I know my wrongdoings,
   my sin is always right in front of me.
I've sinned against you—you alone" (Psalm 51:3-4).

Title: The Rebel People

Our Human Condition:
Because we have the capacity to make choices, we see ourselves as self-sufficient. We become self-centered. And because we want no limits placed on us, we rebel against our Creator in our attempt to take control. Yet we know that there is turmoil in the world and in ourselves, but we don't know why.
Remind the group that "Our Human Condition" reflects the condition of the people in this session's Scriptures, and, as we will see, also reflects conditions of humankind today. Ask participants to underline the part of the human condition they most easily relate to personally.

Opening Prayer: Pray the prayer aloud together from this session in the Study Manual:

"Come back to me and have mercy on me;
   that's only right for those who love your name" (Psalm 119:132).

VIEW THE DVD (5 MINUTES)

EXPLORE "THE REBEL PEOPLE" (30 MINUTES TOTAL)

Share Group Experience: (8 MINUTES)
Divide participants into groups of 4–6 and ask each group to write a definition of *sin*, reflecting on their readings and the information from the DVD.
Ask each group to read their definition of *sin* to the whole group.

Share the Following: (2 MINUTES)
Here is another, perhaps similar, definition of *sin*: "individual or corporate actions or inactions that cause separation from a perfect relationship with God." Let's keep the idea of "separation from a perfect relationship with God" in mind as we work through the session today.

2 THE REBEL PEOPLE

The first eleven chapters of Genesis contain ancient stories passed down through oral tradition. They are theological narratives, told and retold by rabbis, intended to explain beginnings. *Genesis* means "beginning." The stories— Creation (Session 1), Adam and Eve, Cain and Abel, Noah and the Flood, and the tower of Babel—teach us about God, humankind, and the relationship between the two.

Dramatic Reading: Adam and Eve (Genesis 2:15-17; 2:25; and all of Chapter 3) (20 MINUTES)

Lead a dramatic reading of the story of Adam and Eve. Ask for volunteers to read the various parts from their Bibles. (Note: It will be easier if people read from the same translation.) Five readers are needed: Adam, Eve, the serpent, the Lord, and a narrator. Encourage the readers to "ham it up"!

After the dramatic reading, ask the whole group:

What does the story tell us about God?

What does the story tell us about humankind?

What does the story tell us about the relationship between God and humankind?

ENCOURAGE SMALL GROUP DISCUSSION (20 MINUTES)

Divide the class into groups of 4–6. Hand out the Small Group Discussion Guide and ask the groups to spend the next twenty minutes on this activity. (Join one of the small group discussions. There is no need to have groups report their discussions with other groups or to "check up on" discussions.)

CONSIDER THE MARKS OF DISCIPLESHIP (10 MINUTES)

Disciples acknowledge their rebellion, accept responsibility for their sin, and repent.

Remind the group that the "Marks of Discipleship" section emphasizes characteristics or practices of a Christ-follower. The session's "mark" is the disciple's response to "Our Human Condition" found at the beginning of each session.

Have the group turn back to "Our Human Condition" in the Study Manual and read it aloud together. Then have the group turn to the "Mark of Discipleship" printed in italics and read it aloud together.

Share the following:

Repentance is defined as "turning away from sin and turning toward God." Repentance is not simply saying, "I'm sorry," and then repeating the behavior.

Ask a few volunteers to share how they practice repentance in their lives (examples: prayer, confession to another person, Communion).

Ask the group to silently consider places in their lives that call for repentance today.

CLOSE WITH PRAYER (5 MINUTES)

Have the group turn to Session 3 in the Study Manual in preparation for writing their prayer concerns.

Share the following information:

As we journey together through this study, let's strive to grow in our prayer life. It is easy to fill our prayer list with people suffering from illness or injury. These prayers are important, but God is also concerned with our spiritual needs.

I encourage you to pray for one another as you grow spiritually in this study.

For this week, I ask each of you to write down privately where and how you feel God is calling you to repent. Pray for God's help to follow through. Although we do not know each person's specific prayer, we can pray for God to help all members of our group with repentance this week.

Ask a volunteer to close the group session in prayer.

When finished, let your group know that next week's readings are easy to understand but long. Encourage them to keep up daily with the assignments.

2 THE REBEL PEOPLE

SMALL GROUP DISCUSSION GUIDE

(20 MINUTES)

Ask one person to be a timekeeper and plan about 6–7 minutes per story for the discussion. As you discuss the following, you may want to refer to your Bible, the Study Manual, and any study notes to help answer the questions. Complete what your group is able in twenty minutes.

Cain and Abel

1. What does the story tell us about God?

2. Where do you find God's grace in the story?

3. What does the story tell us about humankind?

4. Discuss the type of offerings you give to God. For example, do you give the "first and best" of your talents, your time, or your money, or perhaps what is "left over"?

Noah

1. What does the story tell us about God?

2. Where do you find God's grace in the story?

3. What does the story tell us about humankind?

4. What does the story tell us about the relationship between God and humankind?

Tower of Babel

1. What is the problem in the story?

2. What does the story tell us about God?

3. What does the story tell us about humankind?

4. What does the story tell us about the relationship between God and humankind?

PREPARE FOR THE SESSION

Make enough copies of the Small Group Discussion Guide (pages 17–18) to distribute to groups of 4–6 participants in your class.

WELCOME AND INTRODUCTION (5 MINUTES)

Greet participants and ask: How did you do with your daily reading this week?

Ask participants to open their Study Manuals to Session 3. Direct the group to read aloud together the following:

Theme Word: Covenant

Theme Verse: "I will make of you a great nation and will bless you. I will make your name respected, and you will be a blessing. . . . All the families of the earth will be blessed because of you" (Genesis 12:2-3).

Title: The Called People

Our Human Condition:

We are bewildered, overwhelmed. We search for a way to make sense out of life. We don't know what to do. We don't know how to begin. We yearn for a call that will take us beyond ourselves.

Spend a few moments thinking about your own life. Ponder how God nudges you to do something that takes you beyond yourself. Next to "Our Human Condition" write down a few of your thoughts.

Opening Prayer: Pray the prayer aloud together from this session in the Study Manual:

> "You, LORD my God!
>   You've done so many things—
>   your wonderful deeds and your plans for us—
>   no one can compare with you!
>   If I were to proclaim and talk about all of them,
>   they would be too numerous to count!" (Psalm 40:5).

VIEW THE DVD (5 MINUTES)

EXPLORE "THE CALLED PEOPLE" (15 MINUTES TOTAL)

Share the Following: (4 MINUTES)

As we begin our discussion of the covenant people, let's begin by looking at the map. Turn to the maps in your study Bible, and look at the map tracing Abraham's family's travels. Notice that the path from Ur to Haran to Hebron is in the shape of a crescent; this area is often referred to as "the Fertile Crescent." People had to travel this route, which follows the rivers, to survive. Going straight west through desert from Ur to Hebron would have been impossible. Ur is thought of as the birthplace of civilization. Its location is in modern-day Iraq.

Today, as we think about Abraham and the covenant made between God and him, let's review the life of Abraham through a quick question-and-answer format.

When I ask a question, if an answer comes to your mind, say the answer aloud. (Scripture references are for you, only if needed.)

1. When God calls Abram, what does God promise him in the covenant? (Answer: land, a great nation, and descendants—Genesis 12:1-3; 17:2.)
2. What is Abram to do in response to God's call? (Answer: leave his home and go to an unknown land; be obedient to God—Genesis 12:1; 17:9.)

In pairs, share a time you have felt God calling you to do something. You may want to refer to your ideas you wrote down while we were thinking about the human condition. (4 MINUTES)

In the midst of Abram's journeys, Lot is in trouble in a battle and Abram rescues him. After the victory, Abram gives ten percent of his gain to King Melchizedek (Genesis 14:14-20). In ancient times, the king's share of his subjects' income was ten percent. This is the beginning of the understanding of the tithe. Tithing, or giving ten percent of our earnings to God, is something to consider doing, if we're not already doing so, when going through this study.

When God calls Abram, God promises he will have descendants. But Sarai is still barren. So, becoming impatient with God's promise, Sarai tells Abram to have sex with her servant, Hagar. As a result, Hagar has a son named Ishmael.

In pairs, share a time you were impatient with God and, like Sarai, took things into your own hands to solve. What happened? (4 MINUTES)

Later, three angels visit Abraham and Sarah. Sarah laughs when she overhears the angels telling Abraham they will have a baby (Genesis 18:13-15). But a year later, Sarah and Abraham have a son and name him Isaac.

Sarah is jealous and struggles with Abraham's love for Ishmael, and she insists Abraham send Hagar and Ishmael away. What does God say will happen to Ishmael? (Answer: He will be made a great nation also.) Read Genesis 21:11-13 if needed. Muslims today trace their lineage to Abraham through Ishmael.

In Genesis 22, the Scriptures say Abraham is tested when God orders him to sacrifice Isaac. Abraham obeys, but an angel is sent to spare Isaac. Review the notes in the Study Manual and the study notes in your Bible. What are some ways of understanding the testing of Abraham? Ask for a few participants' thoughts. (3 MINUTES)

Sarah dies. Abraham remarries and has many more children, but the covenant continues through Isaac. Isaac travels to Haran and marries Rebekah.

ENCOURAGE SMALL GROUP DISCUSSION (35 MINUTES)

Divide the class into groups of 4–6. Hand out the Small Group Discussion Guide and ask the groups to spend the next thirty-five minutes on this activity. Ask that one person in each group lead the discussion and another keep time.

CONSIDER THE MARKS OF DISCIPLESHIP (10 MINUTES)

Disciples respond to God's call to enter the covenant community of faith and express commitment to the covenant through the tithe.

Have the group turn to page 28 of the Study Manual and read aloud the paragraph before the "Marks of Discipleship" section. It begins, "So the covenant community is called . . ."

Have the group turn back to "Our Human Condition" in the Study Manual and read it aloud together. Then have the group turn to the "Mark of Discipleship" printed in italics and read it aloud together.

Discuss the first question under "Marks of Discipleship" together as a whole group. What are some marks by which we Christians can tell we are a part of God's community of faith?

Remind the group that the emphasis this week on tithing stems from the Scripture. It is one way to enter into the covenant community of faith.

Divide the group into pairs and have them discuss the remaining questions under the "Marks of Discipleship" section. Have them share as they are comfortable.

CLOSE WITH PRAYER (5 MINUTES)

Ask participants to turn to Session 4 in the Study Manual and write down prayer requests from the group.

Close the group session in prayer.

SMALL GROUP DISCUSSION GUIDE
(35 MINUTES TOTAL)

Review and discuss the stories of Isaac, Jacob, and Joseph using the following outline. Refer to your Bible and study notes. Only look up Scripture references in parentheses if needed.

Isaac and Jacob (15 MINUTES)

1. Isaac's wife, Rebekah, becomes pregnant with twins who fight in the womb. Read aloud Genesis 25:19-26.

2. With help from his mother, Jacob, the younger twin, takes both the birthright (inheritance) and the blessing (also tied to the laws for inheritance) from Esau, the elder twin. Briefly, discuss how Jacob carries out this scheme (Genesis 27).

3. Jacob travels to Haran to escape Esau's anger and to find a wife. On the way, Jacob has a dream. This dream shows the passing of the covenant to Jacob. Read aloud Genesis 28:13-15. In response, Jacob tithes (Genesis 28:20-22).

4. Arriving in Haran, Jacob falls in love with Rachel, his uncle Laban's daughter. He works seven years for the right to marry Rachel, but he is tricked by Laban and marries Leah. Laban allows him to marry Rachel also, but what must Jacob do in return?

5. Rachel is barren and jealous of Leah, who has children. Rachel finally has a son, Joseph.

6. Now wealthy, Jacob leaves Laban to return to his homeland. Jacob prepares to meet Esau, but he is afraid. What does Jacob do in preparation for meeting Esau (Genesis 32)?

7. Then, in the night, Jacob wrestles with God and sees God "face-to-face." What do you think the Scriptures mean when they say Jacob saw God face-to-face (Genesis 32:30)?

8. Jacob's name is changed to Israel. Why is his name changed (Genesis 32:28)?

9. Esau offers Jacob reconciliation (Genesis 33). Discuss these questions: Have you ever been in Jacob's situation, wanting forgiveness and reconciliation but unsure if it will come? How did it feel? How did you prepare? What happened?

10. Jacob returns to his homeland. Rachel gives birth to her second son, Benjamin. She dies in childbirth. Benjamin is Jacob's twelfth son. Because Jacob's name is changed to Israel, these twelve sons' descendants become the twelve tribes of Israel.

Joseph (20 MINUTES)

1. Joseph has dreams and tells his brothers about them. What is the main idea of the dreams? What do the brothers do with Joseph? Where does Joseph end up (Genesis 37)?

2. What happens in Egypt with Potiphar's wife (Genesis 39)?

3. Joseph continues to interpret dreams while in prison. Eventually, Joseph is asked to interpret Pharaoh's dream. Joseph is placed in charge of all of Egypt. He prepares for the famine he has predicted. Ten of Joseph's brothers travel to Egypt for food and end up bowing before Joseph. Eventually, all of Jacob's sons and families end up in Egypt.

4. Read aloud Genesis 50:18-21. Have you ever been able to say words like Joseph's, "You planned something bad for me, but God produced something good from it"?

5. Discuss the two instructions in your Study Manual on the top of page 28. "In looking back over your life, where do you see God's shaping and guiding providence?" and "Recall an experience in your life when God made good come out of evil."

6. Joseph dies around 1700 B.C. The sons of Israel promise that one day Joseph's bones will be taken back to the land where Abraham, Isaac, and Jacob are buried.

4 GOD HEARS THE CRY

PREPARE FOR THE SESSION

Make enough copies of the Small Group Discussion Guide (page 22) to distribute to groups of 4–6 participants in your class.

WELCOME AND INTRODUCTION (5 MINUTES)

Greet participants and ask: How did you do with your daily reading this week?

Ask participants to open their Study Manuals to Session 4. Direct the group to read aloud together the following:

Theme Word: Deliverance

Theme Verse: "I've clearly seen my people oppressed in Egypt. I've heard their cry of injustice because of their slave masters. I know about their pain. I've come down to rescue them from the Egyptians" (Exodus 3:7-8).

Title: God Hears the Cry

Our Human Condition:

Human beings who are humiliated, exploited, or enslaved cry out for deliverance. They wait for a deliverer. They plead, "Does anybody care?"

Point out that the plural form (human beings) is used this week because it is reflective of the weekly Scripture. As participants consider the human condition, ask them to name out loud groups of people in our world today who they feel are humiliated, exploited, or enslaved, and waiting for deliverance.

Opening Prayer: Open in prayer, including the daily prayer from the Study Manual:

"Hear my words, Lord!
  Consider my groans!
    Pay attention to the sound of my cries, my king and my God,
      because I am praying to you!
Lord, in the morning you hear my voice.
In the morning I lay it all out before you.
Then I wait expectantly" (Psalm 5:1-3).

VIEW THE DVD (5 MINUTES)

EXPLORE "GOD HEARS THE CRY" (5 MINUTES)

Share the Following:

Before we begin discussing Moses, let's find the map of the Exodus in the back of your study Bible and get a general idea of the geography of the Exodus.

(Pause to allow participants time to locate and look at the map.)

Remember, God's covenant with Abraham promised him many descendants, land, and a nation. There are many descendants of Abraham, but they have neither land nor their own nation. Now, with the new pharaoh's orders to kill the Hebrew baby boys, it's time for deliverance.

ENCOURAGE SMALL GROUP DISCUSSION (25 MINUTES)

Divide the class into groups of 4–6. Hand out the Small Group Discussion Guide and ask the groups to spend the next twenty-five minutes on this activity.

Share the Following: (20 MINUTES TOTAL)

With the final plague approaching, God gives the Hebrew people exact instructions on how to prepare for it. Each household is to kill a perfect firstborn lamb and put its blood on the sides and top of the door frame, and then eat the lamb with bitter herbs and unleavened bread. They are told to eat quickly with their shoes and coats on, ready to go.

The tenth plague, the plague of death of the firstborn, "passes over" the Hebrew homes marked with blood. The Hebrew children live but the Egyptian firstborns die, including Pharaoh's child. After his child's death, Pharaoh releases the Hebrews.

As the Hebrews leave Egypt, with the wealth of the Egyptians, the Lord guides them into freedom with the pillar of fire by night and the cloud by day. But soon Pharaoh changes his mind and comes after them. The Israelites see the Egyptian forces approaching.

Ask a volunteer to read aloud Exodus 14:10-14, then ask the group to discuss:

Think of a time you felt God was giving you the same message, "Stand your ground, and watch the LORD rescue you today. The LORD will fight for you. You just keep still." In groups of three, share personal experiences. (5 MINUTES)

Next, God parts the sea, and all the Israelites cross safely. The Egyptians follow and drown. Finally, the Hebrew people fear the Lord and put their trust in God and in Moses, God's servant. Soon, however, the people start complaining about not having water or food.

Ask a volunteer to read aloud Exodus 16:2-3, then in groups of three discuss:

Think of a time when you have been freed from a difficult situation. This could be one of many things—a job you hated, a bad relationship, financial debt, an addiction, bad health. Even though you were extremely thankful, how soon did you find yourself complaining in the new situation? In groups of three, share your experiences. (5 MINUTES)

The Hebrew people receive manna from God every day except the day before the Sabbath, when they receive a double portion. What do you think God is trying to teach the people? (Answer: to trust God daily and to observe the Sabbath.)

Think of a time when you literally depended on God's daily provisions. How did that dependence affect your faith? In groups of three, share personal experiences. (5 MINUTES)

In the Exodus story, God makes it clear that God cares about people in bondage.

God specifically teaches the Hebrews and the Egyptians that God is the one true God. God shows that God calls people to be God's servants and messengers of freedom. God teaches that God will fight the battles and will provide for all our needs.

CONSIDER THE MARKS OF DISCIPLESHIP (10 MINUTES)

Disciples hear and obey God's call to be bearers of God's message of deliverance.

Remind the group that the "Marks of Discipleship" section emphasizes characteristics or practices of a Christ-follower. The "mark" is the disciple's response to "Our Human Condition" found at the beginning of each session.

Have the group turn back to "Our Human Condition" in the Study Manual and read it aloud together. Then have the group turn to the "Mark of Discipleship" printed in italics and read it aloud together.

Ask the group:

What are ways we can be bearers of God's message of deliverance?

Would one of you share a personal deliverance story?

(Be prepared to share one of your own if necessary. This could be a story of deliverance from a bad situation, a job, a relationship, a place, an addiction, and so forth.)

CLOSE WITH PRAYER (5 MINUTES)

Ask participants to turn to Lesson 5 in the Study Manual and write down their prayer requests, especially ones that reflect today's theme of deliverance.

Choose an oppressed people in the world to pray for this week.

You may want to ask for a volunteer to close the group session in prayer.

SMALL GROUP DISCUSSION GUIDE
(25 MINUTES TOTAL)

The Beginning of the Story of Moses (5 MINUTES)

Quickly review the basic story of Moses from his birth through the burning bush, using the following prompts. Refer to the Scripture only when needed.

1. What do Shiphrah and Puah, two Hebrew midwives, do in response to the king of Egypt's order to kill the Hebrew baby boys as they are born (Exodus 1:15-22)?

2. What does Moses' mother do when Moses is born (Exodus 2:1-3)?

3. How are Miriam, Moses' sister, and Pharaoh's daughter involved (Exodus 2:4-10)?

Moses is nurtured in his mother's Hebrew faith, trained in the ways of the Egyptian king's court, and educated by the finest scholars in the known world.

4. Later, Moses kills an Egyptian. Why? What happens (Exodus 2:11-15)?

In Midian, Moses marries and has children (Exodus 2:16-21).

5. Moses sees the burning bush. What does God call Moses to do? What does Moses say?

Turn to the "Marks of Discipleship" on pages 36–37 in your Study Manual. Share your answers to 6 and 7 below (also found on page 37 of your Study Manual). (10 MINUTES)

6. The call of Moses is central to Exodus. Describe any times in your life when you have felt God speaking to or calling you.

7. Describe any sense of reluctance you have felt about responding when God called you to a difficult task.

Moses answers the call and then ten plagues are brought upon Egypt. The plagues are: the Nile turns to blood, frogs, gnats, flies, livestock disease, boils, hail, locusts, darkness, and finally, the death of the firstborn. Several times the Scripture says "God hardened Pharaoh's heart" or "made him stubborn"; several times it says "Pharaoh hardened his own heart" or "was stubborn to God."

Pharoah's Hardened Heart (10 MINUTES)

Discuss the following questions. Remember, no one has a monopoly on the "right answer."

1. Why do you think the Bible says God hardened Pharaoh's heart (or "made him stubborn," as the Common English Bible says)? Consider these verses: Exodus 4:21; 7:3-5; and 10:1-2. Read a few of the study notes in your Bible.

2. The Bible also says Pharaoh hardened his own heart (or remained stubborn) (Exodus 7:22). What do you think happened? How and why do you think this happens to people? (The Study Manual suggests, on pages 33–34, "willful resistance to God's intentions makes a person calloused.")

3. What do you think can keep a person from developing a "hardened heart," being stubborn toward God or calloused?

5 GOD SENDS THE LAW

PREPARE FOR THE SESSION

Make enough copies of the Small Group Discussion Guide (page 25) to distribute to groups of 4–6 participants in your class.

WELCOME AND INTRODUCTION (5 MINUTES)

Greet participants and ask: How did you do with your daily reading this week?

Ask participants to open their Study Manuals to Session 5. Direct the group to read aloud together the following:

Theme Word: Order

Theme Verse: "Moses called out to all Israel, saying to them: 'Israel! Listen to the regulations and the case laws that I'm recounting in your hearing right now. Learn them and carefully do them'" (Deuteronomy 5:1).

Title: God Sends the Law

Our Human Condition:

We cannot abide chaos. We want structure. Boundaries give a sense of security. We need order to feel we belong.

Ask participants to write a short phrase reminding themselves of a time in their lives when they were in chaos or a time when they needed boundaries. (These will not be shared.)

Opening Prayer: Open in prayer, including the daily prayer from the Study Manual:

> "LORD, teach me what your statutes are about,
>   and I will guard every part of them.
> Help me understand so I can guard your Instruction
>   and keep it with all my heart.
> Lead me on the trail of your commandments
>   because that is what I want" (Psalm 119:33-35).

VIEW THE DVD (5 MINUTES)

EXPLORE "GOD SENDS THE LAW" (30 MINUTES)

Share the Following:

In Exodus 19, Moses and God talk at Mount Sinai, and God extends the covenant made with Abraham. Ask a volunteer to read aloud Exodus 19:1-8.

Next, Moses heads to Mount Sinai as directed by God. But Moses is away for a long time. It's going on forty days and the people grow restless. Ask the group: What do the people do while Moses is away?

Readers of the Bible are often frustrated with both Aaron's and the people's behavior. Even though Aaron has observed many miracles, he seems to have lost faith in God when he builds an idol to worship. Think of a time when, under great pressure, you or a leader became a crowd pleaser against better judgment, especially when unsure of the support of a higher leader. Perhaps this is what happened to Aaron. Or you may have another idea for his motives. You may also wonder how the people can lose their faith so quickly. Remember, they think Moses might be dead since he is gone so long. It is interesting to ponder this situation. What do you think happened? Discuss as a large group.

When Moses returns and sees the golden calf, what does he do and what does God do?

After several months in the desert, Moses sends twelve spies, one from each tribe, into Canaan, the Promised Land. What do the spies report? What is the result of the story? Ask for responses from the whole group. Refer to Numbers 13:20-24 if necessary.

In this week's reading, we also learn that Moses never gets to enter the Promised Land. Refer to Numbers 20:2-12 if needed.

ENCOURAGE SMALL GROUP DISCUSSION (20 MINUTES)

Divide the class into groups of 4–6. Hand out the Small Group Discussion Guide and ask the groups to spend the next twenty minutes on this activity.

CONSIDER THE MARKS OF DISCIPLESHIP (10 MINUTES)

Disciples keep God's law by doing it.

Have the group turn back to "Our Human Condition" in the Study Manual and read it aloud together. Then have the group turn to the "Mark of Discipleship" printed in italics and read it aloud together.

Divide into pairs and discuss the directions under the "Marks of Discipleship" section.

CLOSE WITH PRAYER (5 MINUTES)

Have the group turn to the next lesson in the Study Manual in preparation for writing their prayer concerns.

Ask a volunteer to close the group session in prayer.

SMALL GROUP DISCUSSION GUIDE
(20 MINUTES)

As you discuss the following, you may want to refer to the Bible, the Study Manual, and any study notes to help answer the questions.

Review silently the Ten Commandments in Exodus 20:1-17. Notice the first three laws demand that we put life completely in God's hands. The next two call for observing Sabbath and showing respect for parents. The last five command against stealing, bearing false witness, and coveting the life and goods of others—all conduct that will destroy community life.

In your Bible readings this week, you have read a portion of the laws. You read food laws, sexual laws, and purification laws, laws concerning diseases, bodily discharges, and a variety of other laws. These laws were added to the Ten Commandments in an effort to interpret them for specific situations.

There are several questions in "The Bible Teaching" section of your Study Manual concerning the laws. As a group, go through these questions and share your answers with one another, as you are comfortable.

Now that you are familiar with the variety of laws, summarize the meaning of the Law by answering these questions:

1. In general, what do you think is the overall purpose of the Law?

2. How do the requirements of the Law make the Israelites a distinct people?

3. What do these laws teach the people about God?

PREPARE FOR THE SESSION

Make enough copies of the Small Group Discussion Guide (page 28) to distribute to groups of 4–6 participants in your class.

WELCOME AND INTRODUCTION (5 MINUTES)

Greet participants and ask: How did you do with your daily reading this week?

Ask participants to open their Study Manuals to Session 6. Direct the group to read aloud together the following:

Theme Word: Atonement

Theme Verse: "A creature's life is in the blood. I have provided you the blood to make reconciliation for your lives on the altar, because the blood reconciles by means of the life" (Leviticus 17:11).

Title: When God Draws Near

Our Human Condition:

When God draws near to us, we feel guilty and ashamed because of our sin. We are overwhelmed by our need of forgiveness when we are in the presence of God. What are we to do?

Ask participants to underline the part of the human condition they most easily relate to personally.

Opening Prayer: Open in prayer, including the daily prayer from the Study Manual:

"I will fulfill my promises to you, God.
I will present thanksgiving offerings to you" (Psalm 56:12).

VIEW THE DVD (5 MINUTES)

EXPLORE "WHEN GOD DRAWS NEAR" (15 MINUTES)

Share the Following:

God has created humankind with an inner need to worship a supreme being. We see it in all cultures from the beginning of time. Now, God's people, as part of the covenant relationship, are given instructions for a specific place and practices for worship. The people are to build a structure that will allow God to dwell among them. The Tabernacle is a portable place of worship. God is clearly present in it, as evidenced by the pillar of fire and the cloud that rises from the Holy of Holies. The Tabernacle is central to all of life.

Exodus 25–27 offers descriptions of the Tabernacle and its furnishings. Locate an image of the Tabernacle and of the Tabernacle furnishings in your study Bible. Try looking around Exodus 25–27 and searching the Web. Notice the detail. What are some of the furnishings mentioned? (Temple furnishings: altar of burnt offering, the laver [washbasin], table of showbread, the lampstand, the altar of incense, the ark of the covenant, the mercy seat.) When reading these chapters, what thoughts came to your mind?

Think about sanctuaries in which you have worshiped. Do you see any similarities to this ancient tabernacle, and if so, what are they?

Once the Tabernacle is finished, instructions are given for worship. Let's look at the three elements of worship individually in our small groups.

ENCOURAGE SMALL GROUP DISCUSSION (30 MINUTES)

Divide the class into groups of 4–6. Hand out the Small Group Discussion Guide and ask the groups to spend the next thirty minutes on this activity.

CONSIDER THE MARKS OF DISCIPLESHIP (10 MINUTES)

Disciples commit themselves to corporate worship.

Have the group turn back to "Our Human Condition" in the Study Manual and read it aloud together. Then have the group turn to the "Mark of Discipleship" printed in italics and read it aloud together.
Ask the group to read silently the paragraphs under the "Marks of Discipleship" section.
Discuss both questions in this section.
In groups of three, discuss: How strong is your commitment to corporate worship?

CLOSE WITH PRAYER (10 MINUTES)

Ask participants to turn to Lesson 7 in the Study Manual in preparation for writing their prayer concerns.
Close the group session in prayer. (This time you could ask each person to say aloud a sentence prayer of thankfulness to God. Examples: "Thank you for worship." "Thank you for loving me.")

SMALL GROUP DISCUSSION GUIDE

(30 MINUTES TOTAL)

God gives the Israelites a specific way to worship that requires remembrance, atonement, and thanksgiving. Discuss each of these elements.

Remembrance (10 MINUTES)

First, the Hebrew people are required to remember. They must never forget their deliverance from Egypt. They are to remember all God has done for them.

1. What do you think is helpful for them about methodically remembering God's faithfulness?

2. Share your answer to the question under "Remembrance" in your Study Manual that says, "What are some of the remembrances you experience when eating the bread and drinking from the cup?"

3. What are other parts of worship that help you remember what God has done for you?

4. How does remembering God's faithfulness strengthen your faith?

Atonement (15 MINUTES)

The second element of worship is atonement (the process of becoming "at one with" God again). God gives the Israelites carefully prescribed worship practices to confess their sins, express their guilt and shame in a community of faith, and make amends directly to the offended one, God, through burnt offerings, often with grain. Animals also are sacrificed. The payment for sin was quite high.

1. How do you think these specific requirements for atonement, which matched the sin with the needed offering, helped the people feel atoned?

2. The Israelites also celebrated and still celebrate the Day of Atonement, Yom Kippur (Leviticus 16, NRSV). What happens on the Day of Atonement? Refer to your Bible reading notes on Day 5 if needed.

3. Share your answer to the directives under "Atonement" in your Study Manual that say, "Explain whether your church's rituals (and which rituals) are helping you feel freed of guilt and shame" and "Explain whether your church's rituals (and which rituals) are helping you feel reconciled to God and neighbor."

4. What other spiritual practices free you of guilt and shame and allow you to feel "at one with" God again?

Thanksgiving (5 MINUTES)

Thanksgiving is the third requirement of worship. It is the offering of gifts to God and God's acceptance of those gifts. The Israelites have prescribed days on the calendar to practice Thanksgiving. They also had special "thank" offerings.

1. Share your answer to the question under "Thanksgiving" in your Study Manual that says, "Today most people have jobs unrelated to agriculture. How can we offer the fruit of our hands in worship and thanksgiving?"

2. How do you offer your thanksgiving to God during worship?

3. What other spiritual practices help you thank God? How about prescribed days, or even holidays, on the calendar?

7 THE PEOPLE WITHOUT A KING

PREPARE FOR THE SESSION

Make enough copies of the Small Group Discussion Guide (pages 32–33) to distribute to groups of 4–6 people in your class.

WELCOME AND INTRODUCTION (5 MINUTES)

Greet participants and ask: How did you do with your daily reading this week?

Ask participants to open their Study Manuals to Session 7. Direct the group to read aloud together the following:

Theme Word: Leadership

Theme Verse: "Then the LORD raised up leaders to rescue them [Israel] from the power of these raiders" (Judges 2:16).

Title: The People Without a King

Our Human Condition:

We cannot tolerate political disorder and confusion. We swing between desiring unity born of faithfulness and wanting to "do our own thing." We need leadership. Please, somebody give us a sense of direction.

Think about times you have desired strong leadership.

Opening Prayer: Pray the prayer aloud together from this session in the Study Manual:

"Rise up, God! Judge the earth
　　because you hold all nations in your
　　　　possession!" (Psalm 82:8).

VIEW THE DVD (5 MINUTES)

EXPLORE "THE PEOPLE WITHOUT A KING" (20 MINUTES TOTAL)

Share the Following:

Summary of the Judges (5 MINUTES)

Let's begin by looking at the map to learn where we are headed when leaving the desert.

Look at the maps in your Bible. Find the map of the conquest of Canaan. Help one another find the east and west shores of the Jordan River, the Sea of Galilee, the Dead Sea, and Jericho.

Notice the size of the entire area. Look at the map of the twelve tribes; see how they settled the land. Remember, the twelve tribes are from the twelve sons of Jacob. You may notice however, that there is no tribe called Joseph. This is because Joseph, who saved his people, is given a double share of land. Instead of one tribe called Joseph, there are two tribes, Ephraim and Manasseh, named after Joseph's sons. However, the land is still divided into twelve tribes, not thirteen, because the Levites (the priests, from the tribe of Levi) have no land.

Instead, there are forty-eight Levite cities spread among the twelve tribes. This way, all twelve tribes have priests.

Joshua (15 MINUTES)

In 1220 B.C., the people leave the wilderness after forty years with Joshua as their leader. They are moving to a new land where other people already live. They do not have a government.

Joshua sends spies into Jericho and Rahab the prostitute helps them. What do the spies and Rahab promise each other (Joshua 2)? (FYI: Rahab is listed in the lineage of Jesus. See Matthew 1:5.)

Who and what lead the crossing of the Jordan (Joshua 3-4)?

What does Joshua have the people do right after they cross the Jordan (Joshua 5:2-10)?

How do the Israelites capture Jericho (Joshua 5–6)?

Read aloud Joshua 24:14-15.
What does it mean to say, "But my family and I will serve the LORD"?

Discuss as a group: What changes, if any, would you make if you were to take this verse very seriously in your own home?

What do you think about Joshua? In your opinion, what makes Joshua a godly leader?

After Joshua dies, next come the judges. In small groups, review three judges.

ENCOURAGE SMALL GROUP DISCUSSION (20 MINUTES)

Divide the class into groups of 4–6. Hand out the Small Group Discussion Guide and ask the groups to spend the next twenty-five minutes on this activity.

CONTINUE TO EXPLORE "THE PEOPLE WITHOUT A KING"
(10 MINUTES)

Summary of the Judges

As the Israelites move into the land, they experience success, but they also have failure. Even with all of God's miracles, laws, and victories, their pattern of living falls into a repeating cycle: Israel sins (often by practicing idol worship), consequences occur (they get attacked or lose battles), Israel repents and begs God for help, and God responds by sending a deliverer (called a judge) and peace comes.

After many rotations of this cycle, chaos takes over. The Book of Judges ends with the people begging for a king who can unite Israel and bring peace.

Perhaps we can understand how this cycle can happen. For example, think of a time you abandoned your faith or a healthy practice or discipline. Then you experienced a negative consequence. Then you repented, asking forgiveness and turning toward God. Finally, you experienced peace. So briefly the cycle is: sin, consequences, repentance and begging for help, peace when help comes.

In pairs, briefly share examples of when you have experienced this cycle in your life.

CONSIDER THE MARKS OF DISCIPLESHIP (10 MINUTES)

Disciples provide a sense of direction and purpose through godly, obedient leadership.

Have the group turn back to "Our Human Condition" in the Study Manual and read it aloud together. Then have the group turn to the "Mark of Discipleship" printed in italics and read it aloud together.

Remind the group that God calls leaders to give people a sense of direction and purpose. When the leaders are godly, they give sound direction. When they are disobedient or ambivalent, they lead people astray.

In groups of three, discuss their responses to their choice of questions in the "Marks of Discipleship" section of the Study Manual.

CLOSE WITH PRAYER (5 MINUTES)

Ask participants to turn to Lesson 8 in the Study Manual and write down their prayer requests.

Ask a volunteer to close the group session in prayer.

SMALL GROUP DISCUSSION GUIDE
(20 MINUTES TOTAL)

Review the high points of the stories of three of the judges: Deborah, Gideon, and Samson.

Deborah (5 MINUTES)

Read aloud Judges 4:1-2.

Deborah was a judge at the time that Jabin, the king of Canaan, ruled over the Israelites. Deborah helped the people settle disputes between one another. But for twenty years Jabin made life miserable for the Israelites.

Finally, the Israelites cried to God for help. In response, Deborah told the commander of Israel's army, Barak, that God would help him defeat Sisera, the head of Jabin's army.

Barak told Deborah that he would go and fight if Deborah would go with him; but if she would not go, then he would not go. What did Deborah say in response (Judges 4:9)?

Then God helped Barak's army kill all of Sisera's men; but Sisera ran away and hid in the tent of Heber the Kenite, whom he thought was an ally.

Jael, Heber's wife, told him that he would be safe inside her tent. Sisera fell asleep. What did Jael do to Sisera while he was sleeping (Judges 4:21)? After this, the Israelites had peace for forty years.

Gideon (5 MINUTES)

Read aloud Judges 6:1.

Where is Gideon when the angel of the Lord calls him (Judges 6:11)?

Where do people normally thresh wheat? What do people normally do in a winepress?

Why do you think Gideon is threshing wheat in a winepress (Judges 6:2-5)?

In a final attempt by Gideon to double-check God's faithfulness and to clarify his calling, Gideon requests what to happen to the wool fleece (Judges 6:36-40)?

Recall a time you "put out a fleece" to God. Take several minutes to share with one another your experiences.

In the end, Gideon wins the battle with only three hundred men.

Samson (10 MINUTES)

Read aloud Judges 13:1.

What was Samson's barren mother told by an angel that her son would do (Judges 13:3-5)?

Samson has trouble with women. He first marries a Philistine woman and starts on a bad path with the Philistines by telling a riddle at his wedding feast. When his new wife betrays him by giving the answer to her people, what does Samson do (Judges 14:19)?

Later, Samson goes back to this wife and tries to go into her bedroom. Her father, who has already given her to someone else in marriage after the wedding feast fiasco, will not let Samson see her. What does Samson do in response (Judges 15:3-8)?

In spite of his flaws, Samson leads Israel for twenty years during the time of the Philistines, even killing one thousand men with a donkey's jawbone.

Eventually, Samson gets involved with his fatal attraction to Delilah. Samson's disobedience and selfish actions are revealed but God remains faithful despite human failure. Before Samson, Israel was in extreme danger of being overtaken by the Philistines. Samson was a key player in saving Israel from them.

When thinking about godly leadership, how do you think a powerful person, with a special godly purpose, falls into disobedience and selfish, destructive behaviors?

PREPARE FOR THE SESSION

Make enough copies of the Small Group Discussion Guide (page 37) to distribute to groups of 4–6 people in your class.

WELCOME AND INTRODUCTION (5 MINUTES)

Greet participants and ask: How did you do with your daily reading this week?

Ask participants to open their Study Manuals to Session 8. Direct the group to read aloud together the following:

Theme Word: Security

Theme Verse: "If you will fear the LORD, worship him, obey him, and not rebel against the LORD's command, and if both you and the king who rules over you follow the LORD your God—all will be well. But if you don't obey the LORD and rebel against the LORD's command, then the LORD's power will go against you and your king to destroy you" (1 Samuel 12:14-15).

Title: The People With a King

Our Human Condition:

We demand leaders, hoping they will bring security and peace. We want our leaders to make decisions for us, to tell us what to do so we won't have to take responsibility for ourselves and our actions. But power tends to corrupt; and we discover our leaders, like us, have feet of clay.

Ask participants to underline the portion of "Our Human Condition" they relate to the most.

Opening Prayer: Pray the prayer aloud together from this session in the Study Manual:

"I will give thanks to you, my LORD,
  among all the peoples;
I will make music to you among the nations
  because your faithful love is as high as heaven;
  your faithfulness reaches the clouds.
Exalt yourself, God, higher than heaven!
Let your glory be over all the earth!" (Psalm 57:9-11).

VIEW THE DVD (5 MINUTES)

EXPLORE "THE PEOPLE WITH A KING" (25 MINUTES TOTAL)

Share the Following:

Today we will briefly cover the stories of Samuel, Saul, David, and Solomon. Let's begin with Samuel. Samuel is the bridge between the judges and the kings.

Samuel (10 MINUTES)

Samuel's mother, Hannah, who is barren, bargains with God. What does she promise God she will do if she has a son (1 Samuel 1:11)?

As a boy, being raised by Eli the priest in the "LORD'S house," Samuel is awakened three times by God in the night but does not recognize God's voice. Then, Eli tells Samuel if God wakes him again, to listen. Samuel receives a message for Eli. What is the message (1 Samuel 3:11-15)?

Samuel grows up and becomes Israel's political and spiritual leader, settling disputes for the people. He constantly urges the Israelites to get rid of idols and only worship the Lord. But when Samuel is an old man, the Jewish leaders take a tough stand and beg Samuel for a king. This hurts Samuel. He feels rejected and that he has failed. Read 1 Samuel 8:7-9 aloud to hear what God says to Samuel in response.

Discuss in groups of three: Share a time when you pleaded with a person or group of people not to do something you felt was wrong or harmful but they chose to reject your advice. How did you feel? What happened in the end?

Samuel warns the people that a king will raise taxes, draft their children, and take their land. But the people persist. So Samuel anoints Saul and later David as kings of Israel. But Samuel never stops warning the people. Read aloud the final verses of Samuel's farewell speech in 1 Samuel 12:24-25.

Saul (10 MINUTES)

Saul, the first king of Israel, is a tall, handsome donkey herder, not excited to be a king. But he starts off as a successful warrior-king winning many battles, especially against the Philistines. However, after David's successful killing of Goliath, the seed of jealously in Saul begins to grow.

Read 1 Samuel 18:6-9 aloud.

Saul, with growing jealousy, paranoia, and fear, becomes focused on ways to kill David. David becomes a fugitive until Saul's death.

Discuss in groups of three: Share times when have you experienced strong feelings of paranoia, jealousy, or fear and it became very difficult to trust God with the situation.

David (5 MINUTES)

Review the story of King David. As I read the following, I will pause in places and ask you to complete the statement out loud.

(Whenever you see ellipses [. . .], pause for participants to respond before proceeding with the italicized answer.)

Samuel anoints David, a shepherd boy, the youngest son of Jesse. David rises to prominence when he kills . . . *the Philistine giant Goliath.*

David soothes Saul with his harp and he becomes best friends with King Saul's son whose name is . . . *Jonathan.*

David writes many songs, which we call the . . . *Psalms.*

David becomes a great leader in Saul's military and in spite of Saul's paranoia, David never tries to kill Saul. David mourns . . . *Saul's death.*

David becomes a great warrior king. He unites the nation and chooses a neutral capital in the city of . . . *Jerusalem.*

David brings to Jerusalem the ark of the covenant, which holds . . . *the Ten Commandments.*

David commits adultery with . . . *Bathsheba* and impregnates her, and then he arranges the death of her husband, . . . *Uriah,* on the battlefield.

David repents with the help of the prophet . . . *Nathan.*

David is king for forty years. He wants to build the Temple, but he is not allowed. David has much blood on his hands and has fought many wars (1 Chronicles 22:6-10). However, he is promised that his son, the next king, will build the Temple. His son's name is . . . *Solomon.*

In spite of his mistakes, David is the king known as a man after God's own heart. He dies and is buried near Jerusalem, in the ancient city of David (1 Kings 2:10).

ENCOURAGE SMALL GROUP DISCUSSION (25 MINUTES)

Divide the class into groups of 4–6. Hand out the Small Group Discussion Guide and ask the groups to spend the next twenty-five minutes on the discussion of David and Solomon.

CONSIDER THE MARKS OF DISCIPLESHIP (10 MINUTES)

Disciples maintain a perspective on leadership that supports and respects godly leaders but give true allegiance only to God.

Have the group turn back to the "Our Human Condition" section in the Study Manual and read it aloud together. Then have the group turn to the "Mark of Discipleship" printed in italics and read it aloud together.

Ask the group: What helps you maintain a healthy perspective of respect and support of leaders? In other words, what helps you to give true allegiance to God and not elevate a human leader to a godly place?

As time allows, choose a few more questions under the "Marks of Discipleship" to discuss.

CLOSE WITH PRAYER (5 MINUTES)

Ask participants to turn to Lesson 9 in the Study Manual and write down their prayer requests, especially with regard to their leaders.

Ask a volunteer to close the group session in prayer.

SMALL GROUP DISCUSSION GUIDE
(25 MINUTES TOTAL)

David (15 MINUTES)

1. How does David's position of power help him to serve God?

2. How does David's position of power encourage him to sin?

3. How does one sin in David's life lead to another?

4. Who is Nathan and what does he tell David (2 Samuel 12:1-12)?

5. How does David respond to the parable (2 Samuel 12:13)?

6. Share times you have experienced a "Nathan" in your life and how you responded. (Think of Nathan as someone who gave you needed correction.)

7. How can David be remembered as one who sought "after God's own heart" when he was also a sinner?

Solomon (10 MINUTES)

Review the story of Solomon.

1. Solomon is anointed the next king. He is known as a wise king and a writer. He is credited with writing most of Proverbs and Ecclesiastes, hundreds of songs, and the Song of Solomon. He becomes extremely wealthy and builds the Temple in Jerusalem.

2. Look for a picture of Solomon's Temple and of the Temple furnishings in your study Bible. It might be located near 1 Kings 6 or search on the Internet. Take a moment to consider the size and the regal qualities of the Temple. Discuss similarities to the mobile Tabernacle the people used at the time of Moses.

3. The Israelites consider the Temple to be God's holy dwelling place among God's people. Read aloud 1 Kings 8:13.

4. The Temple is completed in 958 B.C. and survives for the next 372 years.

5. Thanks to his great warrior-king father, Solomon doesn't have to fight many battles, so he is able to expand the territory and develop international trade. As part of peace treaties and trade deals, he marries many foreign women who worship other gods.

6. Due to the influence of foreign wives, what does Solomon do in his old age (1 Kings 11:4-6)?

7. By the time Solomon dies after his forty-year reign, the Israelites are demanding relief from their high taxes and forced labor. The nation is on the brink of revolt.

8. Solomon is wise and trusts God, but as he becomes more successful, he seems to forget who he is and who God is. How do you think this can happen to a good leader?

9. Share an example when you have allowed negative influences into your personal world, thinking they would be okay and not affect you, but in the end you became influenced by them yourself.

NOTES

PREPARE FOR THE SESSION

Make enough copies of the Small Group Discussion Guide (page 40) to distribute to groups of 4–6 people in your class.

WELCOME AND INTRODUCTION (5 MINUTES)

Greet participants and ask: How did you do with your daily reading this week?

Ask participants to open their Study Manuals to Session 9. Direct the group to read aloud together the following:

Theme Word: Warning

Theme Verse: "The LORD said to me, 'Amos, what do you see?' 'A plumb line,' I said. Then the LORD said, 'See, I am setting a plumb line in the middle of my people Israel. I will never again forgive them'" (Amos 7:8).

Title: God Warns the People

Our Human Condition:

Generally we do not heed warnings until too late. We hate to be told we are doing wrong. We don't really believe that severe punishment will come to us. Leave us alone. We are getting along fine. We will call you when we need you.

Ask participants to reflect silently on a time in their lives when they did not pay attention to a warning.

Opening Prayer: Pray the prayer aloud together from this session in the Study Manual:

"Won't you bring us back to life again
  so that your people can rejoice in you?
Show us your faithful love, LORD!
  Give us your salvation!" (Psalm 85:6-7).

VIEW THE DVD (5 MINUTES)

EXPLORE "GOD WARNS THE PEOPLE" (10 MINUTES)

Share the Following:

Solomon dies, leaving an angry nation that has fallen into idol worship and is burdened by high taxes and conscription. As a result, the kingdom splits. Rehoboam, Solomon's son, becomes the king of the Southern Kingdom, which includes Jerusalem and the Temple. It is called Judah.

The ten northern tribes revolt and choose Jeroboam as their king. The nation is called Israel, and Shechem is its capital. To keep his people from going to Solomon's Temple in Jerusalem for worship, Jeroboam makes houses of worship in Bethel and in Dan, placing a golden calf idol in both. Ask a volunteer to read 1 Kings 12:26-30 aloud.

Find a map of the Divided Kingdom in your Bible and locate the capitals, Jerusalem in the Southern Kingdom (Judah) and Shechem in the Northern

Kingdom (Israel). Also find Bethel and Dan, the new places of worship in the north.

Now, look in your Study Manual at the list of the kings and prophets in the Northern and Southern Kingdoms on page 80. All kings in the northern Jewish nation of Israel are portrayed as godless and evil. All but four in the south are considered evil.

God responds to this crisis by sending prophets. Prophets are called to announce God's words and God's actions. They are strongly opposed to two things—paganism and injustice. The prophets we covered in this session span a time period of nearly 350 years.

ENCOURAGE SMALL GROUP DISCUSSION (40 MINUTES)

Divide the class into groups of 4–6. Hand out the Small Group Discussion Guide and ask the groups to spend the next forty minutes on the discussion of Elijah, Amos, and Isaiah.

CONSIDER THE MARKS OF DISCIPLESHIP (10 MINUTES)

Disciples recognize and listen to prophetic voices raised about community, nation, and world and at times become the prophetic voice.

Have the group turn back to the "Our Human Condition" section in the Study Manual and read it aloud together. Then have the group turn to the "Mark of Discipleship" printed in italics and read it aloud together.

Have the group read in unison the paragraphs under "Marks of Discipleship." Divide the group into pairs and have them discuss the two questions.

CLOSE WITH PRAYER (5 MINUTES)

Ask participants to turn to Lesson 10 in the Study Manual and write down their prayer requests. Suggest they pray prayers this week related to the warnings they need to listen to.

Ask a volunteer to close the group session in prayer.

SMALL GROUP DISCUSSION GUIDE
(40 MINUTES TOTAL)

Review the following stories and answer the questions. Use your daily notes and the Scripture references to review the story only when necessary.

Elijah (15 MINUTES)

Elijah is one of the first prophets. He lives in the Northern Kingdom during the reign of the evil king Ahab. King Ahab is married to a foreign woman, Jezebel, who wants to wipe out Judaism and replace it with her own gods, such as Baal. She tries to kill many Israelite prophets, but some survive. Elijah, who has been out of the area, comes back and challenges all Jezebel's prophets to a duel on Mount Carmel.

1. Retell the story of what happens on Mount Carmel (1 Kings 18–19).

2. Even though God shows God's mighty power on Mount Carmel, Elijah is exhausted and Jezebel is trying to have him killed. What happens to Elijah when he is running from Jezebel?

3. How does God speak to Elijah once he is rested (1 Kings 19:3-19)?

4. Briefly review the story of Naboth's vineyard and the prediction of the death of Ahab and Jezebel (1 Kings 21).

5. What are the sins of Ahab (1 Kings 16:30-33)?

6. What is the basic warning of Elijah?

7. Thinking about paganism and idol worship, if Elijah were speaking to our city today, what would he say? What might he say to you personally? Remember, paganism is anything we put before God in our lives.

Amos (10 MINUTES)

Amos is a prophet in the Northern Kingdom and Southern Kingdom just before the fall of the Northern Kingdom to Assyria.

1. Turn in your Study Manual to review the message of Amos. Share your answers to the three instructions on page 72.

Isaiah (15 MINUTES)

Isaiah is a prophet in the south during the fall of the Northern Kingdom.

1. What is Isaiah's basic message to the people in the chapters you read (Isaiah 1; 3–6)?

2. What is happening in the land during the time he speaks these words?

3. What is Isaiah's vision in Isaiah 6?

4. What does Isaiah say in response to God's question, "Whom shall I send, and who will go for us?" (Isaiah 6:8)?

5. Share in pairs a time when you responded to God's questions, "Whom shall I send, and who will go for us?" with "I'm here; send me."

PREPARE FOR THE SESSION

Make enough copies of the Small Group Discussion Guide (pages 44–45) to distribute to groups of 4–6 people in your class.

WELCOME AND INTRODUCTION (5 MINUTES)

Greet participants and ask: How did you do with your daily reading this week?
Ask participants to open their Study Manuals to Session 10. Direct the group to read aloud together the following:

Theme Word: Consequences

Theme Verse:
"Haven't you brought this on yourself
     by abandoning the LORD your God,
   who has directed your paths?" (Jeremiah 2:17).

Title: God Punishes the People

Our Human Condition:
We think we can sidestep the consequences of our sins, but we cannot.
We deceive ourselves. We think religious practices will save us. We think wealth or prestige will protect us. But we are held accountable. Then we respond to punishment by denying; blaming others; and displaying anger, depression, and despair. Often we refuse comfort and even deny new possibilities. We think all is lost.
Underline the parts that speak to you the most right now.

Opening Prayer: Pray the prayer aloud together from this session in the Study Manual:

"Please, for the sake of your good name,
     LORD, forgive my sins,
   which are many!" (Psalm 25:11).

VIEW THE DVD (5 MINUTES)

EXPLORE "GOD PUNISHES THE PEOPLE" (10 MINUTES)

Share the Following:
Historically this session focuses on the fall of the kingdoms—first, the fall of the Northern Kingdom to the Assyrians in 722–721 B.C., and then the fall of the Southern Kingdom to the Babylonians in 587–586 B.C.
Look at the maps of the Assyrian and Babylonian empires found at the back of your study Bible. Note the vast size of the empires.
Think about the fall of the Northern Kingdom, Israel, to the Assyrians. Remember that every king in the Northern Kingdom is described as one who did evil in the sight of the Lord. King Ahab introduced Baal worship to them.
Ask a volunteer to read 1 Kings 16:30-33 aloud.

The last king in the Northern Kingdom was Hoshea, who was not only evil but also a traitor.

Ask a volunteer to read 2 Kings 17:4-6 aloud.

The small wars with Syria and Edom, Ammon and Philistia, gave way to war on a huge scale. The ruthless and cruel Assyrians laid siege on the Northern Kingdom of Israel for three years and finally it fell. The Assyrians marched them away into captivity in 722 B.C.

Ask participants to silently reread 2 Kings 17:7-23 or look at their daily notes to remind them why God allowed the kingdom to fall. Ask the class for a brief answer to the question.

ENCOURAGE SMALL GROUP DISCUSSION (35 MINUTES)

Divide the class into groups of 4–6. Hand out the Small Group Discussion Guide and ask the groups to spend the next thirty-five minutes on the discussion.

CONTINUE EXPLORING "GOD PUNISHES THE PEOPLE"
(5 MINUTES)

Share the Following:

We understand the sin and the consequences of the people. We see how God uses prophets to speak to the people words of warning. But, in the midst of all the warning and the suffering, we also hear the prophets speak God's words of comfort.

Jeremiah writes one of the most comforting and encouraging passages in the Bible, even in the midst of these horrific times.

Ask for a volunteer to read aloud one of Jeremiah's laments, Lamentations 3:22-23.

Many times we cannot see that ray of hope when our world crashes in. We think revenge rather than repentance.

Can you see how the people in exile could feel hopeless? But the prophets also said words of comfort. Read aloud Isaiah 40:1-2; Isaiah 43:1-2; and Isaiah 49:15-16.

We also read the words of Ezekiel. He is a priest who is exiled early from Jerusalem to Babylon.

In exile, he becomes a prophet. He spends half of the book telling the people that God is going to let the Babylonians destroy Jerusalem. He spends the second half of the book giving the people hope and the message that God is with them and will eventually send them back to Jerusalem to rebuild their nation to a level of glory they have never seen.

We read part of the opening vision he has in Chapters 1 and 2 resulting in a new, life-changing understanding of God.

What is the main point of the story of Ezekiel's vision in Ezekiel 1? Refer to your Study Manual, if necessary. (Answer: Ezekiel's vision offers new understanding. Even with the Temple destroyed, without Jerusalem, in exile, in punishment, even in Babylon, God is everywhere. God is with the people, even in exile. This is a major shift of theological understanding. People begin worshiping God, even in exile.)

10 GOD PUNISHES THE PEOPLE

CONSIDER THE MARKS OF DISCIPLESHIP (10 MINUTES)

Disciples accept the consequences of their sin, seek forgiveness, and look for healing and new opportunities for faithfulness. Disciples choose to serve rather than to despair when suffering the consequences of sin.

Have the group turn back to the "Our Human Condition" section in the Study Manual and read it aloud together. Then have the group turn to the "Mark of Discipleship" printed in italics and read it aloud together.

Discuss in pairs two questions: When you are in the midst of suffering the consequences of your sin, how have you also experienced comfort? Have you been able to serve others?

CLOSE WITH PRAYER (5 MINUTES)

Ask participants to turn to Lesson 11 in the Study Manual and write down their prayer requests. Suggest they pray prayers this week related to the warnings they need to listen to.

Ask a volunteer to close the group session in prayer.

SMALL GROUP DISCUSSION GUIDE
(35 MINUTES)

1. The Northern Kingdom falls but the Southern Kingdom, Judah, lasts about 135 years longer before falling to the Babylonian Empire. This is largely due to a few good and faithful kings. We read about one faithful king, Josiah.

2. King Josiah follows the forty-five-year reign of the evil King Manasseh. By this time in history, the Babylonian Empire has conquered the Assyrian Empire and the Babylonians are threatening the Southern Kingdom, Judah.

3. What does King Josiah do to try to save the kingdom? (Refer to 2 Kings 22:1-2; 2 Kings 23; and your daily notes and the Study Manual, if needed.)

4. The prophets appeared during the time of the kings of Israel and Judah. The prophets brought God's message to a rebellious people who had forsaken the Lord.

5. Jeremiah is a prophet of the Southern Kingdom. He comes on the scene at the end of Josiah's reign. He is a young boy when God chooses him. He not only predicts the worst disaster possible, but he lives to see it.

6. Look at your daily notes from reading Jeremiah. What is the main idea you hear from Jeremiah?

7. Read Jeremiah 2:13 and Jeremiah 9:13-16 aloud.

8. Jeremiah prophesies for over forty years, beginning in the reign of Josiah and continuing until after the fall of Jerusalem. He writes Lamentations, a description of the nearly three-year siege Babylon puts on Jerusalem. Read Lamentations 4:4-14 aloud.

9. After this punishing siege, Jerusalem comes under horrendous attack and the magnificent city, including God's dwelling place, the Temple, becomes a pile of stones. Many are killed and the remaining are exiled except for the very poor, who are left.

10. Jeremiah cries out over the destruction of the Temple and the city of Jerusalem.

11. Try to imagine the devastation. Recall that the Temple, for the last 372 years, is where the people believe God lived. Can you imagine how the people can now believe their God is dead or has been conquered by the Babylonian gods? Consequences have occurred. All is lost.

12. The Bible is clear about the sin of the people and the consequences. Discuss the following:

    a) How do you feel about the consequences that God allowed to happen to both Israel and Judah?

    b) Share experiences when you were held strictly accountable and received the consequences of your actions.

    c) We have choices of how we respond to consequences. Share examples of when you have been willing to accept the consequences of your sin, seek forgiveness, and look for healing.

11 GOD RESPONDS TO THE PEOPLE

PREPARE FOR THE SESSION

Your group will be doing a dramatic reading this week. Prepare giant nametags that identify the role of each reader. You will need a label for Job, Eliphaz, Bildad, Zophar, Elihu, and the Lord. Make enough copies of "A Reader's Play of Job" at the end of this lesson (pages 50–52) for each person in your group. The readers will use it as their script and the class will follow along, making notes for discussion.

Discuss and plan with your group a gathering to celebrate the completion of the Old Testament portion of this study.

WELCOME AND INTRODUCTION (5 MINUTES)

Greet participants and ask: How did you do with your daily reading this week?

Ask participants to open their Study Manuals to Session 11. Direct the group to read aloud together the following:

Theme Word: Wisdom

Theme Verse: "Turn your ear toward wisdom, / and stretch your mind toward understanding. / Call out for insight, / and cry aloud for understanding. / Seek it like silver; / search for it like hidden treasure. / Then you will understand the fear of the LORD, / and discover the knowledge of God. / The LORD gives wisdom; / from his mouth come knowledge and understanding" (Proverbs 2:2-6).

Title: God Responds to the People

Our Human Condition:

We have questions about God and life. We hide parts of ourselves—certain feelings and thoughts—from God, ourselves, and others. We want to be healthy and happy, but on our own terms. Often we are not willing to pay the price that right living requires. Life isn't fair. Sometimes the wicked prosper and the good are cut down. Suffering bewilders us. Why did this happen? We need answers from God.

Ask participants to underline the parts of "Our Human Condition" they most easily relate to personally.

Opening Prayer: Pray the prayer aloud together from this session in the Study Manual:

"LORD, you have examined me.
  You know me.
You know when I sit down and when I stand up.
  Even from far away, you comprehend my plans.
You study my traveling and resting.
  You are thoroughly familiar with all my ways" (Psalm 139:1-3).

11 GOD RESPONDS TO THE PEOPLE

VIEW THE DVD (5 MINUTES)

EXPLORE "GOD RESPONDS TO THE PEOPLE" (20 MINUTES TOTAL)

Share the Following: (10 MINUTES)
Psalms

In this session we will look at the Wisdom Literature found in the Psalms, Proverbs, and the Book of Job.

As we look at the Psalms, we remember the Israelites are in exile. Ezekiel has shared his powerful vision that God is everywhere. The people are worshiping in small groups in foreign lands.

Although the Psalms were written over hundreds of years, they are especially important to the people in exile because the people were able to take these written songs with them in their hearts.

Divide the class into groups of 3–4. Ask participants to spend ten minutes discussing their answers to the questions in this week's readings that cover the Psalms. Remind them to share only what they are comfortable sharing. Hopefully you will see that throughout history, people have trusted God with all their thoughts and feelings.

Share the Following: (10 MINUTES)
Proverbs

History continues as we read from Ezra and Nehemiah.

Remember, in 539 B.C. the powerful Babylonian Empire is overtaken by the massive Persian Empire, which stretches from India to Egypt and Libya. Cyrus, the Persian king, issues a decree that all Babylonian exiles can return to their homelands. King Cyrus encourages the Jews to rebuild their Temple, and he sends gold and silver and even returns the Temple furnishings that had been stolen.

Some Jews choose to stay in exile, but many do return, and they return in at least four waves. When they complete the Temple in Jerusalem in 515 B.C., it is nothing like Solomon's elegant structure. But this Temple lasts for the next five hundred years. This is the Temple Jesus will worship in. In the third wave of exiles returning, Ezra the priest returns to teach God's laws to the Jews.

Ezra prays, asking God to forgive the people for their disobedience. He urges people to follow the Law, including divorcing their foreign wives and sending them and their children away. Although this is controversial, many do. The people return to keeping the Sabbath. They take care of the Temple, let the land rest, cancel all debts every seventh year, tithe, and pay the Temple tax. The Jews do not want to repeat their recent, tragic history. They strive to live in harmony with God's laws even though obedience is costly. The people hold strong beliefs that the ways of God are good. Following these ways lead to a healthy, harmonious life. Evil ways lead to destruction.

In preparation for this session, you read a variety of proverbs. In pairs, spend five minutes discussing your impressions about the proverbs you read. Share one area in your life you feel God is calling you to "right living."

11 GOD RESPONDS TO THE PEOPLE

Share the Following: (35 MINUTES TOTAL)
Job (5 MINUTES)

After studying Proverbs and Ezra and Nehemiah, we can see that the strong theology during this postexilic period of Jewish history is that "right living brings reward." After all, the people had suffered terribly for wrongdoing. It is easy to see that right living brings blessing and peace. However, what about when bad things happen to good and faithful people? The story of Job addresses this difficult theological question.

To understand Job, we must remember that at this time in Jewish history, the understanding of Satan is that he "is not the enemy of God but a kind of official accuser, a member of the heavenly council." (See the Study Manual, page 92.) This explanation of Satan helps us understand the dialogue between Satan and God in the prologue. Here, the author of Job is establishing that Job is a perfect, faithful man. This fact is crucial to understanding the theological point of the story. We are not to doubt that part of the story. Think of the prologue between God and Satan as a setup for the story so the author can make the theological points needed. It is the author's way of establishing the predicament.

Dramatic Reading of Job (10 MINUTES)

Ask for volunteers who enjoy dramatic reading to take a part in "A Reader's Play of Job." You will need participants to read six parts: Job, Eliphaz, Bildad, Zophar, Elihu, and the Lord. Hand out scripts to the entire class and a nametag for each reader. Encourage them to read with emotion! Have participants listen for and mark the kinds of counsel Job's friends offer him.

Large Group Discussion (10 MINUTES)

After the reading, ask the group the following questions:
1. What are the kinds of counsel offered by Job's friends? (Nobody is perfect; You, your children, or somebody sinned; You are being disciplined; Trust God; God will help you; Don't be angry with God; Shut up; You have no right to complain; Trouble comes to everybody.)
2. Which ones do you feel are helpful, if any?
3. What happens to Job that changes his attitude toward God? In other words, what makes Job able to rest from his questions and find peace?
4. Read aloud the last four lines Job speaks in the play (Job 42:5-6): "In the past I knew only what others had told me, / but now I have seen you with my own eyes. / So I am ashamed of all I have said / and repent in dust and ashes." Ask the whole group: What do you think Job experienced that caused him to say "but now I have seen you with my own eyes"? Listen to a few answers.

Share the Following: (10 MINUTES)

Certainly Job experiences a powerful personal encounter with God that is so real, Job has no doubts it is God, and it forever changes him. Personal encounters with God happen in many ways. People tell of hearing a word, song, sermon, or message from an old friend that was perfectly timed for what they needed. Others share seeing a rainbow at an exact time they needed reassurance of God's presence, seeing a bird appear and stay near them at a special time, finding themselves in a circumstance that was miraculous, hearing an audible voice, or experiencing a visit by an angel.

Sometimes people do not share these experiences because they are so powerful and such personal faith-builders that people do not want anyone else to lessen their experience. However, when these experiences are shared, they can be great encouragement for others.

Divide the class into pairs or groups of three. Ask participants to share, as they are able, any stories they have of their own powerful encounters with God. Remind them that when people share these experiences, they are very personal and meaningful. The circumstances behind the encounters are not necessary to share; we are interested in the actual encounter.

CONSIDER THE MARKS OF DISCIPLESHIP (5 MINUTES)

Disciples trust God with all their thoughts and feelings, strive to live in harmony with God's laws, and trust God in the face of unexplained suffering.

Have the group turn back to the "Our Human Condition" section in the Study Manual and read it aloud together. Then have the group turn to the "Mark of Discipleship" printed in italics and read it aloud together.

Divide the group into pairs to discuss the "Marks of Discipleship" section. Are you able to embrace all of the "Mark of Discipleship"? If not, which part is the most difficult and why?

CLOSE WITH PRAYER (5 MINUTES)

Ask participants to turn to Lesson 12 in the Study Manual and write down their prayer requests. Suggest they pray for one another in areas where trusting God is the most difficult.

Ask a volunteer to close the group session in prayer.

11 GOD RESPONDS TO THE PEOPLE

A READER'S PLAY OF JOB

JOB: O God, put a curse on the day I was born;
  put a curse on the night when I was
   conceived! . . .
 I wish I had died in my mother's womb
  or died the moment I was born. . . .
 I have no peace, no rest,
  and my troubles never end.

ELIPHAZ: You have taught many people
  and given strength to feeble hands. . . .
 Now it's your turn to be in trouble,
  and you are too stunned to face it.
 You worshiped God, and your life was
  blameless;
  and so you should have confidence
  and hope.
 Think back now. Name a single case
  where someone righteous met with
   disaster.
 I have seen people plow fields of evil
  and plant wickedness like seed;
  now they harvest wickedness and evil. . . .
 "Can anyone be righteous in the sight of God
 No indeed! We bring trouble on ourselves,
  as surely as sparks fly up from a fire.
 If I were you, I would turn to God
  and present my case to him. . . .
 Happy is the person whom God corrects!
  Do not resent it when he rebukes you. . . .

JOB: Why won't God give me what I ask?
  Why won't he answer my prayer?
 If only he would go ahead and kill me!
 If I knew he would, I would leap for joy,
  no matter how great my pain.
 I know that God is holy;
  I have never opposed what he commands. . . .
 But you think I am lying—
  you think I can't tell right from wrong. . . .

JOB: (*to God*): Remember, O God, my life is only
  a breath. . . .
 I am angry and bitter. . . .
 Why are people so important to you? . . .
 Are you harmed by my sin, you jailer?
  Why use me for your target practice?

BILDAD: God never twists justice;
  he never fails to do what is right.
 Your children must have sinned against God,
  and so he punished them as they deserved.
 But turn now and plead with Almighty God. . .
  then God will come and help you
  and restore your household as your reward.

JOB: But how can a human being win his case
  against God? . . .
 God is so wise and powerful;
  no one can stand up against him. . . .
 Though I am innocent, all I can do
  is beg for mercy from God my judge. . . .
 Isn't my life almost over? Leave me alone!

ZOPHAR: God is punishing you less than you
  deserve. . . .
 God knows which people are worthless;
  he sees all their evil deeds. . . .
 Put your heart right, Job. Reach out to God.
 Put away evil and wrong from your home. . . .
  God will protect you and give you rest. . . .

JOB: Even my friends laugh at me now. . . .
  although I am righteous and blameless;
  but there was a time when God
   answered my prayers.
 You have no troubles, and yet you make
  fun of me. . . .
 I am ready to state my case,
  because I know I am in the right.
 Are you coming to accuse me, God?
  If you do, I am ready to be silent and die.
 Let me ask for two things; agree to them,
  and I will not try to hide from you;
  stop punishing me, and don't crush me
   with terror.
 Speak first, O God, and I will answer.
  Or let me speak, and you answer me.
 What are my sins? What wrongs have I done?

ELIPHAZ: No one who is wise would . . . defend himself
  with such meaningless words.
 If you had your way, no one would fear
  God. . . .

11 GOD RESPONDS TO THE PEOPLE

Your wickedness is evident by what you say; . . .
   you are condemned by every word you
      speak. . . .
Why, God does not trust even his angels;
   even they are not pure in his sight.
And we drink evil as if it were water;
   yes, we are corrupt; we are worthless. . . .

JOB: (*to God*) You have worn me out, God;
   you have let my family be killed.
I am skin and bones,
   and people take that as proof of my
      guilt. . . .

BILDAD: You are only hurting yourself with
      your anger.
   Will the earth be deserted because you
      are angry?
The light of the wicked will still be put out;
   its flame will never burn again. . . .

JOB: You think you are better than I am,
   and regard my troubles as proof of my guilt.
Can't you see it is God who has done
      this? . . .
Why must you persecute me the way God
      does? . . .
But I know there is someone in heaven
   who will come at last to my defense.
Even after my skin is eaten by disease,
   while still in this body I will see God. . .
   and he will not be a stranger. . . .
When I think of what has happened to me,
   I am stunned, and I tremble and shake.
Why does God let evil people live,
   let them grow old and prosper?
They have children and grandchildren,
   and live to watch them all grow up.
God does not bring disaster on their homes;
   they never have to live in terror. . . .

ELIPHAZ: Is there anyone, even the wisest,
   who could ever be of use to God?
Does your doing right benefit God,
   or does your being good help him at all?
It is not because you stand in awe of God
   that he reprimands you and brings you
      to trial.

No, it's because you have sinned so much;
   it's because of all the evil you do. . . .

JOB: I still rebel and complain against God . . . .
How I wish I knew where to find him,
I would state my case before him . . . .
I want to know what he would say . . . .
I follow faithfully the road he chooses,
   and never wander to either side.
I always do what God commands;
   I follow his will, not my own desires. . . .
   I tremble with fear before him. . . .

BILDAD: Can anyone be righteous or pure in
      God's sight?
In his eyes even the moon is not bright,
   or the stars pure.
   What is a human life worth in God's eyes? . . .

JOB: If only my life could once again
   be as it was when God watched over
      me. . . .
I have always acted justly and fairly.
I was eyes for the blind,
   and feet for the lame.
I was like a father to the poor
   and took the side of strangers in trouble.
I destroyed the power of cruel men
   and rescued their victims. . . .
Why do you attack a ruined man,
   one who can do nothing but beg for
      pity? . . .
I swear I have never acted wickedly
   and never tried to deceive others.
Let God weigh me on honest scales,
   and he will see how innocent I am. . . .

ELIHU: . . . It is the spirit of Almighty God
   that comes to us and gives us wisdom.
It is not growing old that makes us wise
   or helps us to know what is right. . . .
Now this is what I heard you say:
"I am not guilty; I have done nothing wrong.
   I am innocent and free from sin.
But God finds excuses for attacking me
   and treats me like an enemy. . . ."
But I tell you, Job, you are wrong.
   God is greater than any human being.

11 GOD RESPONDS TO THE PEOPLE

Why do you accuse God
   of never answering our complaints?
Although God speaks again and again,
   no one pays attention to what he says. . . .
God speaks to make them stop their sinning
   and to save them from becoming proud.
He will not let them be destroyed;
   he saves them from death itself.
God corrects us by sending sickness
   and filling our bodies with pain. . . .
God does all this again and again;
   each one saves a person's life,
   and gives him the joy of living. . . .
God's power is so great that we cannot
     come near him;
   he is righteous and just in his dealings
     with us. . . .

THE LORD (*to Job*): Who are you to question my
     wisdom
   with your ignorant, empty words?
Now stand up straight
   and answer the questions I ask you.
Were you there when I made the world?
   If you know so much, tell me about it.
Who decided how large it would be?
   Who stretched the measuring line over it?
   Do you know all the answers?

What holds up the pillars that support
     the earth?
   Who laid the cornerstone of the world? . . .
Job, you challenged Almighty God;
   will you give up now, or will you answer?

JOB: I spoke foolishly, Lord. What can I
     answer? . . .
   I know, Lord, that you are all-powerful;
     that you can do everything you want.
You ask how I dare question your wisdom
   when I am so very ignorant.
I talked about things I did not understand,
   about marvels too great for me to know.
You told me to listen while you spoke
   and to try to answer your questions.
In the past I knew only what others had
     told me,
   but now I have seen you with my own eyes.
So I am ashamed of all I have said
   and repent in dust and ashes.

*(This play is excerpted from the Good News
Translation in Today's English Version [GNT].)*

12 PEOPLE HOPE FOR A SAVIOR

PREPARE FOR THE SESSION

Make enough copies of the Small Group Discussion Guide (page 56) to distribute to groups of 4–6 people in your class.

Make sure all participants know about any event planned to celebrate the completion of the Old Testament and when the New Testament sessions begin.

WELCOME AND INTRODUCTION (5 MINUTES)

Greet participants and ask: How did you do with your daily reading this week?

Ask participants to open their Study Manuals to Session 12. Direct the group to read aloud together the following:

Theme Word: Hope

Theme Verse: "Look, I am sending my messenger who will clear the path before me; suddenly the LORD whom you are seeking will come to his temple. The messenger of the covenant in whom you take delight is coming, says the LORD of heavenly forces" (Malachi 3:1).

Title: People Hope for a Savior

Our Human Condition:

We swing between two extremes. Either we drift into cynicism, supposing that evil prospers and death ends all, or we try to convince ourselves that a new government, a change in leadership, or some quick fix will save us. Only special people seem to catch the vision of God's final kingdom of peace. We need and desire something more. So we wait.

Read aloud together. Ask participants to underline the part of the "Our Human Condition" section they relate to in their lives right now. In addition, think about an area of your life that you desire something more, something to change.

Opening Prayer: Pray the prayer aloud together from this session in the Study Manual:

> "God! My God! It's you—
> I search for you!
> My whole being thirsts for you!
> My body desires you
> in a dry and tired land,
> no water anywhere" (Psalm 63:1).

VIEW THE DVD (5 MINUTES)

EXPLORE "PEOPLE HOPE FOR A SAVIOR"

Share the Following:

We've just heard an overview of the history of the Jews from the Persian Empire to the mighty Roman Empire when Christ is born. The Jews experienced horrible persecution during this time. One source of encouragement to the Israelites during these years is the story of Daniel.

ENCOURAGE SMALL GROUP DISCUSSION (25 MINUTES TOTAL)

Divide the class into groups of 4–6. Hand out the Small Group Discussion Guide and ask the groups to spend the next twenty-five minutes on this activity.

Share the Following: (5 MINUTES)
Daniel

Daniel 7–12 is apocalyptic, visionary, and symbolic. In your Study Manual, you learned the definitions of *apocalyptic literature*. At this point in our study of the Scriptures, perhaps the most important understanding of apocalyptic literature is that it gives reassurance that God is ultimately in control. Daniel's visions describe conflict and involve both earthly and heavenly figures. They give the Jews of the second century B.C. confidence and hope. We can also gain hope when we draw on these ancient apocalyptic visions of God's victory.

Discuss in pairs: When you think of Daniel's vision, what spiritual truths come to your mind?

Do you live in hope of God's final victory, believing that God's kingdom will endure forever?

Share the Following: (15 MINUTES)
Jonah

We know the Jews were strictly following the law in the years between Ezra and the time of Jesus. They were, in many ways, living separate from others. But what about the ultimate purpose of God's covenant people—to be God's light to the world?

Perhaps that is why we have the story of Jonah.

Ask the group for quick, short answers to the following questions. Use the Scripture references only if needed.

1. What does God ask Jonah, a Jewish prophet, to do and how does Jonah respond (Jonah 1:1-2)?
2. What happens on the ship (Jonah 1:3-14)?
3. How would you briefly paraphrase Jonah's prayer from the belly of the fish (Jonah 1:17-2:10)?
4. What does Jonah say to the people in Nineveh and how do they respond (Jonah 3:4-9)?
5. How does Jonah react to their repentance (Jonah 4:1-3)?
6. What is the point of the shade tree at the end (Jonah 4:10-11)?

In pairs discuss where or who is your personal Nineveh. In other words, what group of people or what specific person would be the hardest for you to tell about the love and grace of God?

12 PEOPLE HOPE FOR A SAVIOR

CONSIDER THE MARKS OF DISCIPLESHIP (15 MINUTES)

Disciples hear the gospel of Jesus Christ in the context of unity with the historic people of God.

Imagine how easy it would be to withdraw, to be bitter, to feel like Jonah, or to wonder if God has completely forgotten you. Can you imagine the Jews' desire for a Messiah, a Savior who would stop all the years of persecution and put an end to the suffering, secure the boundaries, and finally let God's people live in peace? So how do people hold on to hope? How do these people make it?

They have the words of hope from many of the prophets foretelling what is to come. In their time of waiting—for peace, for a solution to their suffering, for a Messiah—they hold on to two thousand years of stories of their ancestors, their psalms of prayer and praise, and their prophecies of hope.

We have discussed that the Jews are waiting for a Savior. Now let's think about our own lives.

Divide the group into pairs. Ask each person to share with their partner something they are waiting or longing for in their own life. (5 MINUTES)

During long periods of waiting, the Hebrew people found strength in the ancient words of the prophets. Hopefully, after spending twelve weeks reading the Old Testament, we are sensing our unity with the Hebrew people, their human conditions, their longings for things to change, and ultimately their hope for a Messiah.

Have the group turn back to "Our Human Condition" in the Study Manual and read it aloud together. Then have the group turn to the "Mark of Discipleship" printed in italics and read it aloud together.

Ask a few volunteers to read aloud their answers to the question under the "Marks of Discipleship."

CLOSE WITH PRAYER (5 MINUTES)

In closing our session today, as Christians we understand the longing for the ultimate kingdom of Christ. But in our waiting, we, like the Hebrews of old, gain strength from the same ancient words of hope from the prophets. We understand our connection to the covenant people of the Old Testament.

Let's now gather in a large circle for our closing prayer.

Assign these prophetic Scriptures to different participants and ask them to read aloud during the prayer when asked: Daniel 2:44; Daniel 7:27; Isaiah 9:6-7; Isaiah 11:6; Zechariah 9:9; and Revelation 11:15.

Have the entire group stand and form a large circle, holding hands.

Thank God for this amazing journey together and offer other appropriate prayers. Then, while still in prayer, ask that the Scriptures be read one after another, in any order.

SMALL GROUP DISCUSSION GUIDE

(25 MINUTES TOTAL)

Review the high points of the stories of Daniel. Refer to your daily notes and Scriptures only if needed.

Daniel and His Friends (10 MINUTES)

Daniel and his friends are taken into the king's court because they are from Judah's royal family. They are handsome and smart. The king is training them for his service. How do the young men live out faithfulness to God during this training (Daniel 1:8-16)?

Discuss what religious practices you would continue to observe if you were put in this situation.

After three years, Daniel and his friends are "ten times better than all the magicians and enchanters in the king's entire kingdom" and they are put into King Nebuchadnezzar's service.
Later, King Nebuchadnezzar has a dream and wants his advisors to tell him both what he dreamed and what the dream means. No one can do this until Daniel. Daniel tells and interprets the dream and gives credit to God for giving him the information. After this, the king elevates Daniel to ruler and chief administrator over Babylon.
Eventually, Nebuchadnezzar makes an idol and decrees that it be worshiped. How do Shadrach, Meshach, and Abednego respond (Daniel 3)?

What happens to them (Daniel 3)?

Daniel in the Lions' Den (5 MINUTES)

Retell briefly the story of Daniel in the lions' den using your daily notes (Daniel 6).

Reflection (10 MINUTES)

Reflecting on these stories, think about the Jews who lived hundreds of years after Daniel under the terrible persecution of Antiochus Epiphanes IV. How did hearing these stories offer them hope?

Still today, many people suffer extreme religious persecution. How do you think you would respond to this type of persecution?

Imagine finding strength from the story of Daniel during a time you are trying to hold on to your faith. What might you say to yourself?

Share your own faith stories or experiences you draw upon for endurance when life is tough and faith is hard.

DISCIPLE

FAST TRACK

NEW TESTAMENT

1 RADICAL DISCIPLESHIP

PREPARE FOR THE SESSION

If you have new people in the New Testament portion of your class, prepare and make enough copies of a group roster (include names and contact information) to hand out to each participant at the beginning of this session.

Make enough copies of the Small Group Discussion Guide (page 61) to distribute to groups of 4–6 people in your class.

WELCOME AND INTRODUCTION (5 MINUTES)

Introduce new participants and hand out the group roster, if applicable.

Greet participants and ask: How did you do with your daily reading for this week?

Ask participants to open their Study Manuals to Session 1. Direct the group to read aloud together the following:

Theme Word: Disciple

Theme Verse: "As Jesus continued on from there, he saw a man named Matthew sitting at a kiosk for collecting taxes. He said to him, 'Follow me,' and he got up and followed him" (Matthew 9:9).

Title: Radical Discipleship

Our Human Condition:

We are anxious. We conform to our culture, knowing all the while that it is sick and riddled with brokenness and confusion. Jesus is a constant threat to our established ways. His lifestyle conflicts with our values. We hope he will go away; but when he keeps coming on, we reject, ridicule, and finally crucify him.

Remind participants that "Our Human Condition" is a statement of who we are as it is described in the week's Scripture readings. Ask participants to silently consider ways we conform to the culture even when it conflicts with our religious understanding.

Opening Prayer: Pray the prayer aloud together from this session in the Study Manual:

"Turn my heart to your laws,
    not to greedy gain.
Turn my eyes away from looking at
      worthless things.
    Make me live by your way.
Confirm your promise to your servant—
    the promise that is for all those who honor you"
                    (Psalm 119:36-38).

VIEW THE DVD (5 MINUTES)

EXPLORE "RADICAL DISCIPLESHIP" (30 MINUTES TOTAL)

Share the Following:

In Matthew, a key emphasis is that Jesus asks people to turn away from "worldly living" and go in a new kingdom or godly direction. This was and still is radical thinking and teaching. It requires total commitment, often going directly against our nature, the current culture, and sometimes even against our religious understandings and traditions.

Divide into four groups (2–4 in each group) and assign each group one of the following Scripture passages from the Sermon on the Mount: Matthew 5:1-26; Matthew 5:27–6:18; Matthew 6:19-38; Matthew 7:1-28. (If working with large DISCIPLE groups, have each table divide themselves into four groups and then share at their table only.)

Ask each group to identify from their section of Scripture two or three examples of the radical discipleship called for by Jesus. In other words, find examples of how followers of Jesus are to live their lives even when it goes against their selfish nature, culture, and/or religious understandings. Remind the group to keep in mind the Old Testament laws, the legalism of the time, and how Jesus is contradicting some of the current understandings. (10 MINUTES)

Invite each group to share examples with the whole class. (5 MINUTES)

Ask the whole group: What is radical about the discipleship that Jesus calls for today? In other words, what are examples of ways that followers of Jesus are to live their lives today that go against our selfish nature, culture, and possibly our religious understandings? Ask for examples. (5 MINUTES)

Read aloud this paragraph from the "Marks of Discipleship" in the Study Manual (page 13): "Can you see how often the church makes discipleship seem too easy? 'Accept Jesus Christ as your Lord and Savior' is so true but often superficial, lacking the radical demands, the total commitment of discipleship: Give up everything and follow Jesus."

Divide the group into pairs and have them discuss this question from their Study Manual: "Describe where you are in your discipleship. Have you responded to Christ's call, 'Follow me'? Is anything or anyone holding you back?" Explain. (10 MINUTES)

ENCOURAGE SMALL GROUP DISCUSSION (20 MINUTES)

Share the Following:

As we read Matthew, we understand that the rejection of Jesus begins very early. Herod seeks to take his life. Then, as Jesus teaches and heals people, the tension mounts, especially among the legalistic leaders of the Pharisees and the wealthy Sadducees who made up the Sanhedrin (the ruling body of the Jews).

In your small groups, work to understand how value clashes, religious controversy, and political conflicts led to the crucifixion of Jesus.

Divide the class into groups of 4–6. Hand out the Small Group Discussion Guide and ask the groups to spend the next twenty minutes on this activity.

CONSIDER THE MARKS OF DISCIPLESHIP (10 MINUTES)

Disciples accept Christ's call to radical discipleship, abandoning sham and pretense, becoming vulnerable, and entering the ministry of making disciples.

Divide the group into pairs and have them discuss this question under the "Marks of Discipleship" on page 14. "In what areas of your life does Jesus continue to threaten your values, your lifestyle?"

Direct the group to look briefly at the special assignment on page 15. Ask participants to bring some ideas to next week's class along with a plan to do something they have never done before. Perhaps someone could plan a field trip in which other interested classmates could participate.

CLOSE WITH PRAYER (5 MINUTES)

Have the group turn to the next lesson in the Study Manual to write their prayer concerns.

Close the group session with prayer.

SMALL GROUP DISCUSSION GUIDE
(20 MINUTES)

As you discuss the following, you may want to refer to the Bible, the Study Manual, and any study notes to help answer the questions.

1. Together review your daily readings and notes and look for 6–8 examples of where Jesus and his teachings and actions clash with the culture, values, and religious understandings, especially of the legalistic, law-following sect of Jews called the Pharisees and the wealthy, powerful sect of Jews called the Sadducees.

How do you think Jesus' radical message and actions contributed to the Crucifixion?

2. Read Matthew 16:24-25: "All who want to come after me must say no to themselves, take up their cross, and follow me. All who want to save their lives will lose them. But all who lose their lives because of me will find them."

What do you think Jesus means when he says to those who want to follow, "All must say no to themselves, take up their cross, and follow me"?

PREPARE FOR THE SESSION

Read through this session and notice under "Explore the Hidden Messiah" the recap of Jesus' life. Be prepared to lead this quickly, allowing the group to fill in your pauses.

WELCOME AND INTRODUCTION (10 MINUTES)

Greet participants and ask: How did you do with your daily reading for this session?

Ask for ideas about the special assignment mentioned at the end of last week's class (from page 15 of the Study Manual). Have the class make a quick plan to follow through, or suggest that individuals discuss this after class. Encourage everyone to try to do something.

Ask participants to open their Study Manuals to Session 2. Direct the group to read aloud together the following:

Theme Words: Good News

Theme Verse: "Now is the time! Here comes God's kingdom! Change your hearts and lives, and trust this good news!" (Mark 1:15).

Title: The Hidden Messiah

Our Human Condition:
Like the disciples, we do not understand who Jesus is. Sometimes we half understand, or misunderstand, or refuse to understand. We especially close our eyes and ears to his call for *self-denial* and *suffering*. This "good news" sounds like bad news to us.

Ask participants to circle a phrase in "Our Human Condition" that challenges them.

Opening Prayer: Pray the prayer aloud together from this session in the Study Manual:

> "God, your way is holiness!
>   Who is as great a god as you, God?
> You are the God who works wonders;
>   you have demonstrated your strength among all peoples"
> (Psalm 77:13-14).

VIEW THE DVD (5 MINUTES)

EXPLORE "THE HIDDEN MESSIAH" (10 MINUTES TOTAL)

Share the Following: (5 MINUTES)
Now that you have read Matthew and Mark, two accounts of Jesus' life, let's highlight key events together. When I pause, say aloud the answer that comes to your mind.

(Whenever you see ellipses [. . .], pause for participants to respond before proceeding with the italicized answer.)

Jesus is born in . . . *Bethlehem.*
The family escapes to Egypt because of Herod's threat to . . . *kill all Jewish children under age two.*
After Herod dies, Mary, Joseph, and Jesus return and live in . . . *Nazareth.*
In Luke, we will read that Jesus visits the Temple in Jerusalem as a boy for . . . *the Passover.*
Later, Jesus is baptized in the Jordan River by his cousin named . . . *John the Baptist.*
Before beginning his ministry, Jesus goes to the wilderness for forty days and is tempted by . . . *Satan.*
In John, we will read that in Cana, Jesus performs his first miracle, which is . . . *turning water into wine.*
Soon, Jesus attracts his first four followers: Peter, Andrew, and the sons of Zebedee, James and John. They all earn their living as . . . *fishermen.*
Jesus begins his first preaching trip near the Sea of . . . *Galilee.*
Matthew decides to follow him. Matthew works as a . . . *tax collector.*
Jesus officially chooses the twelve disciples.
Jesus preaches the Sermon on the Mount. The sermon includes the Beatitudes, the Lord's Prayer, and many other teachings.
Jesus sends the twelve disciples out to preach and heal.
John the Baptist is killed by . . . *King Herod.*
Jesus feeds the five thousand, walks on water, and feeds the four thousand.
Peter says Jesus is the Son of God.
Jesus tells the disciples he is going to die soon.
He is transfigured in front of . . . *Peter, James, and John.*
In John, he raises from the dead his friend . . . *Lazarus.*
Jesus predicts his death and resurrection.

In his last week, Jesus makes his "triumphal" entry to Jerusalem, clears the Temple, teaches in the Temple, and oversees the Passover meal (we now refer to that event as the Last Supper). Judas betrays him, and, as predicted, Peter denies him three times. Also as predicted, Jesus is arrested, tried, crucified, and buried. On the third day, he is resurrected. Jesus appears to his followers several times before his final ascension into heaven.

Share the Following: (5 MINUTES)
Mark identifies Jesus as the Christ, the Son of God. In Hebrew, *Christ* means "Messiah," or "one who has been anointed." Mark presents Jesus as one who tries to keep his messianic identity secret. Yet the more Jesus says to keep quiet, the more people proclaim his miraculous deeds.
It isn't until Jesus' trial before the Sanhedrin (the highest Jewish ruling council, made up of powerful Pharisees and Sadducees) that he makes his identity known. When he does, he is condemned to death.
Ask the group: Why do you think Jesus wanted to keep his identity a secret?

ENCOURAGE SMALL GROUP DISCUSSION (25 MINUTES)

Divide the class into groups of 4–6. Have participants turn to page 19 of the Study Manual and read the second paragraph together aloud (beginning with "When Jesus preached or . . ."), then have each group continue through the Bible Teaching section, discussing the stories and questions.

CONSIDER THE MARKS OF DISCIPLESHIP (15 MINUTES)

Disciples understand their ministry as a call to self-denial and suffering.

Have the group turn back to "Our Human Condition" in the Study Manual and read it aloud together. Then have the group turn to the "Mark of Discipleship" printed in italics and read it aloud together.
Ask the group: What does a call to self-denial and suffering look like to you?

Divide the class into groups of three and have them discuss their responses to the second and third points under the "Marks of Discipleship" on page 23.
Remind participants of the special assignment on page 15 of the Study Manual. Reiterate your encouragement to try to do something. Participants may want to stay after the session to discuss the assignment.

CLOSE WITH PRAYER (5 MINUTES)

Have the group turn to the next lesson in the Study Manual in preparation for writing their prayer concerns.
Close the group session in prayer.

3 GOD SEEKS THE LEAST, THE LAST, AND THE LOST

PREPARE FOR THE SESSION

Make enough copies of the Small Group Discussion Guide (page 68) to distribute to groups of 4–6 people in your class.

WELCOME AND INTRODUCTION (5 MINUTES)

Greet participants and ask: How did you do with your daily reading this week?

Ask if anyone followed through on the special assignment from last week. If anyone has, ask for a brief report.

Ask participants to open their Study Manuals to Session 3. Direct the group to read aloud together the following:

Theme Word: Least

Theme Verses:
"The Spirit of the Lord is upon me,
    because the Lord has anointed me.
He has sent me to preach good news to the poor,
    to proclaim release to the prisoners
    and recovery of sight to the blind,
    to liberate the oppressed,
    and to proclaim the year of the Lord's favor" (Luke 4:18-19).

Title: God Seeks the Least, the Last, and the Lost

Our Human Condition:
I don't really like the poor. They're not always clean. I stay away from sick people. They smell bad. I don't understand people whose customs, culture, and ways of thinking are different from mine. They make me feel uncomfortable. I don't want to go to church with them or socialize with them. People with disabilities also make me feel awkward. Actually, I enjoy being with people who are just like me.

Ask participants to underline the statement in "Our Human Condition" that is most like them.

Opening Prayer: Pray the prayer aloud together from this session in the Study Manual:

"I'm poor and needy.
    Hurry to me, God!
You are my helper and my deliverer.
    Oh, LORD, don't delay!" (Psalm 70:5).

VIEW THE DVD (5 MINUTES)

3 GOD SEEKS THE LEAST, THE LAST, AND THE LOST

EXPLORE "GOD SEEKS THE LEAST, THE LAST, AND THE LOST" (5 MINUTES)

Share the Following:

Luke, a physician and a fellow worker with the apostle Paul, was the only non-Jew to write any of the books of the Bible. He writes both Luke and Acts.

Biblical scholars believe he wrote both Luke and Acts because in the Book of Acts there is a shift from third person to first person in reporting Paul's later travels. For example: "We prepared to leave for the province of Macedonia" (Acts 16:10).

Luke 15 is often referred to as "God's Lost and Found Department" because it contains the stories of the lost sheep, the lost coin, and the lost son. Luke records the attention Jesus gives to women. Luke traces Jesus' family tree back to Adam. Luke's Gospel is meant for all, Jews and Gentiles. Luke emphasizes that the risen Christ is both a call for repentance and an offer of forgiveness.

Ask the whole group: Suppose you had never heard about Jesus. What did you learn about Jesus from Luke's Gospel?

ENCOURAGE SMALL GROUP DISCUSSION (30 MINUTES)

The Gospel of Luke contains the largest number of parables (twenty-four), fourteen of which are not told in the other Synoptic Gospels. Twentieth-century theologian William Barclay points out that the parables of Jesus use familiar examples to lead our minds toward heavenly concepts, calling each "an earthly story with a heavenly meaning."

Divide the class into groups of 4–6. Hand out the Small Group Discussion Guide and ask the groups to spend the next 30 minutes on this activity.

Share the Following:

The Good Samaritan (15 MINUTES)

Samaria is the region of the Northern Kingdom that falls to the Assyrians in 722 B.C. The conquering Assyrian pioneers who settle in the region marry Jewish survivors, mixing the races and the religions. These people become known as Samaritans, and the "pure" Jews grow to hate them. The region forms a huge geographical block between Galilee in the north and Jerusalem in the south. Most Jews avoid this area even though the detour around it is lengthy and the road treacherous. The road in the story, between Jerusalem and Jericho, is seventeen miles long and drops 3,300 feet. It is narrow, rocky, and difficult to travel on.

Have everyone turn in their Bibles and quickly review Luke 10:25-37.

Say the following about the characters in the story:

1. The priest, a religious leader: Touching a corpse would mean losing his turn of duties at the Temple (Numbers 19:11). He refuses to risk that.
2. The Levite, a religious layperson: Robbers often use decoys, like a wounded man, to trick people. Perhaps the Levite wants to play it safe. Or perhaps he is in a hurry.

3. The Samaritan, the hated foreigner: The original listeners to the parable would have thought the villain has arrived.

Discuss the following questions:

> What is the key question that is asked in this story and who asked it?

> What is Jesus telling us in the story?

Divide into groups of three and discuss: Who do you find difficult to treat as a neighbor? Why? Explain.

CONSIDER THE MARKS OF DISCIPLESHIP (10 MINUTES)

Disciples throw their weight with God's mission to the least, the last, the lost.

Have the group turn back to "Our Human Condition" in the Study Manual and read it aloud together. Then have the group turn to the "Mark of Discipleship" printed in italics and read it aloud together.

Divide the group into threes and have them discuss their responses to the questions on pages 30–31.

CLOSE WITH PRAYER (5 MINUTES)

Ask participants to turn to the next session in the Study Manual and write down their prayer requests.

Close the group session in prayer.

3 GOD SEEKS THE LEAST, THE LAST, AND THE LOST

SMALL GROUP DISCUSSION GUIDE
(30 MINUTES TOTAL)

Parables in Luke (10 MINUTES)

Choose parables from the following list of some parables unique to Luke (other than those from Luke 15). Read each one aloud and discuss what you think the point of the parable is. Be sure to read the study notes in your Bible for additional information. (Discuss as many as you can in ten minutes.)

- The friend at night (Luke 11:5-8)

- Lowest seat at the feast (Luke 14:7-14)

- The great banquet (Luke 14:16-24)

- Counting the cost (Luke 14:28-33)

- The unjust judge (Luke 18:2-8)

- The Pharisee and the tax collector (Luke 18:10-14)

Luke 15: The Lost Sheep, Lost Coin, and Lost Son (20 MINUTES)

Read aloud Luke 15:1-7, the lost sheep. Discuss the following:

1. Who or what is lost and how did it get lost?

2. Share several personal examples of times you have gotten lost in the same way.

3. What does the parable tell us about God?

4. What does the parable tell us about humankind?

5. What does the parable tell us about the relationship between God and humankind?

Read aloud Luke 15:8-10, the lost coin. Discuss the questions above.

Read silently Luke 15:11-31, the lost son. Discuss the questions above.

As you discovered in each parable, something is lost, though for different reasons. Each time, when something or someone is found, it is celebrated. God's love reaches all who are lost, regardless of the reason, and celebrates all who are found.

4 LIFEGIVER

PREPARE FOR THE SESSION

Make enough copies of the Small Group Discussion Guide (page 72) for Session 4 to distribute to groups of 4–6 people in your class.

WELCOME AND INTRODUCTION
(5 MINUTES)

Greet participants and ask: How did you do with your daily reading this week?
Ask participants to open their Study Manuals to Session 4. Direct the group to read aloud together the following:

Theme Word: Life

Theme Verse: "I came so that they could have life—indeed, so that they could live life to the fullest" (John 10:10).

Title: Lifegiver

Our Human Condition:
Most of the time life seems meaningless. What is the point of living? I try to get close to others, but often I feel cut off. How can I live a happy, productive life, at peace with myself and others? I want more than religion or religious ceremony. I want to experience God as a living presence in my life. I want to live with spiritual power.
Ask participants to think of a time when they have felt one of the emotions in this human condition.

Opening Prayer: Pray the prayer aloud together from this session in the Study Manual:

"How precious, O God, is your constant love!
    We find protection under the shadow of your wings.
We feast on the abundant food you provide;
    you let us drink from the river of your goodness.
You are the source of all life,
    and because of your light we see the light"
                (Psalm 36:7-9, GNT).

VIEW THE DVD (5 MINUTES)

EXPLORE "LIFEGIVER" (35 MINUTES TOTAL)

Share the Following: (5 MINUTES)
John, the beloved disciple of Christ, emphasizes the following in the Gospel of John:

- what it means to live life with Jesus as Savior and Lord
- the inner assurance of abundant and eternal life given to believers through the Holy Spirit

To begin our discussion, let's look at how Jesus often describes himself. He uses symbols that are life-sustaining, such as bread, water, and light.

Ask the whole group: With his references to life-sustaining symbols, what do you think Jesus wants people to realize and understand about him?

Dramatic Reading (10 MINUTES)

Jesus and Nicodemus (John 3:1-21)

Lead a dramatic reading of Nicodemus's encounter with Jesus in John's Gospel. Recruit volunteers to read the various parts from their Bibles. (Note: It will be easier if people read from the same translation.) Three readers are needed: Jesus, Nicodemus, and the narrator.

After reading, ask the group:

1. What do we know about Nicodemus?
2. Why do you think Nicodemus comes to see Jesus at night?
3. What does Nicodemus want to know?
4. In pairs, considering the Scripture you just heard, discuss: How would you answer someone if they asked you, "What must I do to be born again?"

Large Group Discussion (5 MINUTES)

Ask the group to recall the story of Jesus and the woman at the well (John 4:1-30).

You will remember that Jesus asks a Samaritan woman, isolated from her own village, for a drink of water. When Jesus reveals what he knows about her and declares that he is the Messiah, the woman experiences complete joy and change in her life.

What do you think happened to the woman that changed her life?

Large Group Discussion (10 MINUTES)

Ask the group to recall the story of Jesus, Mary, and Martha (John 11:1-44).

You will remember that in this story, Jesus' friend Lazarus is ill. Lazarus's sisters send for Jesus, but Jesus comes after Lazarus has been dead four days. Jesus raises Lazarus from the dead. Jesus says, "I am the resurrection and the life. Whoever believes in me will live, even though they die. Everyone who lives and believes in me will never die" (John 11:25-26).

Ask the group:

1. How do you think the resurrection of Lazarus affected Mary and Martha's view of Jesus?
2. Still today, people experience miracles during sickness and/or death. Have you, or someone you know, had a meaningful faith experience, perhaps even a conversion to Christ, in the midst of sickness or even the death of a loved one? Briefly share your story.

Share the Following: (5 MINUTES)

In these stories and many others, John wants us to know that with Christ, one can live life on earth "to the fullest," meaning with purpose, hope, peace, joy, love, forgiveness, direction, security, eternal life, and much more. Jesus brings life into the "inside" of a person where meaninglessness resides. This kind of life is not a gift after death but a gift to the believer now. John is telling us that life with Christ is different than life without Christ.

4 LIFEGIVER

In pairs share how you responded to the instruction in your Study Manual (page 38) that says, "Try, in your own words, to describe the 'life' you have found in Jesus Christ." If you are not sure, talk about the life you are longing for and what might be holding you back from receiving it.

ENCOURAGE SMALL GROUP DISCUSSION (15 MINUTES)

In the Gospel of John, we also learn more about the Holy Spirit than in the other three Gospels combined. John says that inner assurance of abundant and eternal life is given to believers through the Holy Spirit.

Divide the class into groups of 4–6. Hand out the Small Group Discussion Guide and ask the groups to spend the next fifteen minutes on this activity.

CONSIDER THE MARKS OF DISCIPLESHIP (10 MINUTES)

Disciples experience life in Jesus Christ and have the inner assurance of abundant, eternal life.

Have the group turn back to "Our Human Condition" in the Study Manual and read it aloud together. Then have the group turn to the "Mark of Discipleship" printed in italics and read it aloud together.

Read aloud the first paragraph under the "Marks of Discipleship." Ask 2–3 volunteers to share how they responded to, "Try, in your own words, to describe the 'life' you have found in Jesus Christ."

Then divide the group into pairs and have them share with each other the responses they gave to the following questions on page 39: "Do you have a sense of assurance? How would you describe your feelings?" and "What meaning, what purpose does your life have in Christ?"

CLOSE WITH PRAYER (5 MINUTES TOTAL)

Ask participants to turn to the next session in the Study Manual and write down their prayer requests.

Close the group session with the following prayer:

Dear God, thank you for the Book of John, which so clearly explains who Jesus and the Holy Spirit are. Thank you for sending us your Son, Jesus Christ. Thank you for sending us an advocate, the Holy Spirit. For any in our group who have not formally accepted your love and forgiveness, or for those of us who desire to surrender even more of ourselves to you, please hear this prayer as we pray together: Lord, I desire to completely surrender myself to you. Forgive me for going my own way. I thank you for forgiving me, loving me, and desiring to be in a relationship with me. I turn my whole life over to you. Through Christ we pray. Amen.

SMALL GROUP DISCUSSION GUIDE
(15 MINUTES)

As you discuss the following, you may want to refer to the Bible, the Study Manual, and any study notes to help answer the questions.

As a group, briefly discuss: When you hear the words *the Holy Spirit*, what comes to your mind?

Read aloud the following about the Holy Spirit:

- John the Baptist says, "I baptize you with water; but he will baptize you with the Holy Spirit" (Mark 1:8).

- In John 14–17, Jesus is at the Last Supper. He prepares the disciples for life in his absence when he teaches them about the Holy Spirit. Jesus explains that with the gift of the Holy Spirit, all believers will have access to him after he is gone.

- One can think of the Holy Spirit as Jesus remaining in us, for comfort and for strength. Some think of the Holy Spirit as the conduit for God to communicate with us.

- Let's remember that the Holy Spirit is never in conflict with God or Jesus. All the attributes we give to Jesus (counselor, guide, comforter, friend, advocate, truth, love, and so forth) we also can give to the Holy Spirit.

Jesus Promises the "Companion"

- Read aloud John 14:15-18, 25-27. Answer the questions in your small group.

    1. What are the main ideas you get from these passages?

    2. How do you experience the Holy Spirit in your life?

The Vine and the Branches

- Read aloud John 15:1-9. Answer the questions in your small group.

    3. Read again verse 5. What does it mean when Jesus says, "If you remain in me and I in you, then you will produce much fruit"?

    4. Jesus says several times in John that he will live "in" his followers. What does it mean to you to believe Jesus lives within you?

5 THE EXPLOSIVE POWER OF THE SPIRIT

PREPARE FOR THE SESSION

Make enough copies of the Small Group Discussion Guide (pages 75–76) for Session 5 to distribute to groups of 4–6 people in your class.

WELCOME AND INTRODUCTION (5 MINUTES)

Greet participants and ask: How did you do with your daily reading this week?

Ask participants to open their Study Manuals to Session 5. Direct the group to read aloud together the following:

Theme Word: Power

Theme Verse: "Rather, you will receive power when the Holy Spirit has come upon you, and you will be my witnesses in Jerusalem, in all Judea and Samaria, and to the end of the earth" (Acts 1:8).

Title: The Explosive Power of the Spirit

Our Human Condition:

We believe in God, but we have so little power. We want to witness, to heal, to convert, to serve, to change society; but we are ordinary people. We lack spiritual vitality.

Ask participants to circle the word or words in "Our Human Condition" to which they most relate.

Opening Prayer: Pray the prayer aloud together from this session in the Study Manual:

"Let God grant us grace and bless us;
    let God make his face shine on us,
    so that your way becomes known on earth,
    so that your salvation becomes known
        among all the nations" (Psalm 67:1-2).

VIEW THE DVD (5 MINUTES)

EXPLORE "THE EXPLOSIVE POWER OF THE SPIRIT"
(20 MINUTES TOTAL)

Share the Following:

Acts is the sequel to the Gospel of Luke. It tells the story of what happens after Jesus ascends into heaven. It describes a dynamic, explosive world where the Spirit of the risen Jesus is active.

The story of Acts covers more than thirty years, from the ascension of Jesus in about A.D. 30 to the trial of Paul in the 60s.

Acts 1:8 sets the theme for the whole Book of Acts: "You will receive power when the Holy Spirit has come upon you, and you will be my witnesses in Jerusalem, in all Judea and Samaria, and to the end of the earth." Luke spends

5 THE EXPLOSIVE POWER OF THE SPIRIT

the rest of the book showing how Jesus' followers are empowered by the Holy Spirit as they witness to the Lord Jesus, even in the midst of opposition and conflict.

Before we begin looking at the stories in Acts, let's talk about Pentecost. Jesus taught clearly that the Holy Spirit would come to all the believers, not just the disciples. Jesus told them to wait for it. Then, the Spirit came upon them "like the howling of a fierce wind" and "individual flames of fire" (Acts 2:2-3). This experience gave them the spiritual power and the physical drive to take the gospel to the world.

Ask the whole group: How do you think people today experience the presence and the power of the Holy Spirit? (5 MINUTES)

Ask the group to share personal examples of experiencing the presence of the Holy Spirit and/or the power of the Holy Spirit. (5 MINUTES)

Look briefly at the maps of the four journeys of Paul in your Bibles. When looking at these maps, trace the movement of Christianity into the Gentile world. Notice how with each journey Paul goes further from Jerusalem. (3 MINUTES)

ENCOURAGE SMALL GROUP DISCUSSION (30 MINUTES)

Divide the class into groups of 4–6. Hand out the Small Group Discussion Guide and ask the groups to spend the next thirty minutes on this activity.

CONSIDER THE MARKS OF DISCIPLESHIP (10 MINUTES)

Disciples experience the presence and the power of the Holy Spirit in their lives and witness to others in order to lead them to Jesus.

Have the group turn back to "Our Human Condition" in the Study Manual and read it aloud together. Then have the group turn to the "Mark of Discipleship" printed in italics and read it aloud together.

In pairs, share your answer to the questions under the "Marks of Discipleship" in your Study Manual.

Then say to your group: "The Holy Spirit gave power to followers to lead others to Christ. Let's each think about three people the Holy Spirit may be urging us to begin to pray for and invite into Christian fellowship."

CLOSE WITH PRAYER (5 MINUTES)

Ask participants to turn to the next session in the Study Manual and write down their prayer requests.

Write the names of three people you are praying for and consider inviting them to worship.

Close the group session in prayer.

5 THE EXPLOSIVE POWER OF THE SPIRIT

SMALL GROUP DISCUSSION GUIDE
(30 MINUTES)

You have read about many powerful events in the first half of Acts this week. You have read about the explosive power of the Holy Spirit to spread the gospel message throughout the known world. Time will not allow a review of all the events in these chapters, but let's discuss those listed below. Focus specifically on how the Holy Spirit gave power to the disciples and changed the lives of others.

Assign someone in your small group as timekeeper to ensure you spend only 6–7 minutes per event.

As you discuss the following, you may want to refer to the Bible, the Study Manual, and any study notes to help answer the questions.

Discussion Questions for Each Event

1. What happens in the event? (Use your daily notes to remind you. Look for Scripture only if needed.)

2. How are the people's lives and/or attitudes changed?

3. Where do you see the action of the Holy Spirit?

4. What do they do with the Holy Spirit's power?

Events in Acts

- Stephen—his choosing, his speech before the Sanhedrin, his stoning (Acts 6–7).

- Philip and the Ethiopian eunuch (Acts 8:26-40). Not only is this convert Ethiopian, he is also powerful. He is in charge of the Ethiopian treasury and so is probably the second in command behind the queen. Many historians think that Judaism spread to Ethiopia during the reign of King Solomon. But regardless of how he has heard of God and Judaism, it is clear that the Ethiopian eunuch is reading the scroll of Isaiah. And now, with his conversion, Christianity spreads to the continent of Africa.

- Saul's conversion (Acts 9). Consider the answers you wrote in your Study Manual on page 45 as you discuss Saul (Paul).

- Cornelius calls for Peter; Peter's vision at Joppa; Peter at Cornelius's house (Acts 10–11). Two key points to consider as you go through the discussion questions:

  1. The end result of Peter's dream (review your answer about the meaning of Peter's vision on page 46 in your Study Manual).

2. The Holy Spirit can still give believers new understandings. As you go through this story, fully consider how life-changing Peter's dream is for him. Remember, Peter is still a law-abiding Jewish man. At this point in history, all Christ-followers are following the laws of Judaism. Can you imagine what a change Peter goes through when he hears the voice of Jesus say, "Never consider unclean what God has made pure" (Acts 10:15). This vision dramatically influences the rules for Gentiles converting to Christianity. At the Jerusalem Council, the decision is made that Gentiles are no longer required to follow all the Jewish law. Some call this story Peter's second conversion, meaning that after we accept Christ for our initial conversion, the Holy Spirit can give us new understandings that may even challenge our previous biblical or religious beliefs.

Have you ever had a "second conversion"? Share with your group your experiences.

6 THE GOSPEL PENETRATES THE WORLD

PREPARE FOR THE SESSION

Make enough copies of the Small Group Discussion Guide (pages 80–81) for Session 6 to distribute to groups of 4–6 people in your class.

WELCOME AND INTRODUCTION (5 MINUTES)

Greet participants and ask: How did you do with your daily reading this week?

Ask participants to open their Study Manuals to Session 6. Direct the group to read aloud together the following:

Theme Word: Conversion

Theme Verse: "You know I have testified to both Jews and Greeks that they must change their hearts and lives as they turn to God and have faith in our Lord Jesus" (Acts 20:21).

Title: The Gospel Penetrates the World

Our Human Condition:

We are uncomfortable witnessing about our faith to strangers and people of different religions. Even with our families and next-door neighbors we hesitate to talk about God. We suspect that people will resent ideas that challenge their beliefs or customs. Besides, we're not sure we would want them to join us.

Ask participants to circle the phrases in "Our Human Condition" they most easily relate to.

Opening Prayer: Pray the prayer aloud together from this session in the Study Manual.

> "But me? I will sing of your strength!
>   In the morning I will shout out loud
>   about your faithful love
>   because you have been my stronghold,
>   my shelter when I was distraught.
> I will sing praises to you, my strength,
>   because God is my stronghold,
>   my loving God" (Psalm 59:16-17).

VIEW THE DVD (5 MINUTES)

EXPLORE "THE GOSPEL PENETRATES THE WORLD"

Share the Following:

The task of first-generation Christians is difficult. Most have not been outside their own villages, and the message they carry is hard for others to comprehend. However, persecution forces these early Christians beyond Jerusalem and causes the spread of the gospel.

ENCOURAGE SMALL GROUP DISCUSSION (40 MINUTES)

Divide the class into groups of 4–6. Hand out the Small Group Discussion Guide and ask the groups to spend the next forty minutes on this activity.

Share the Following: (10 MINUTES)

Many times toward the end of his third journey, Paul is warned not to return to Jerusalem. He returns anyway, saying, "But nothing, not even my life, is more important than my completing my mission. This is nothing other than the ministry I received from the Lord Jesus: to testify about the good news of God's grace" (Acts 20:24). The sequence and nature of the events reported in Acts 21:15–28:31 are as follows:

Paul arrives in Jerusalem in A.D. 57 with the offering money for the Christ-following community. He is warmly received. However, Paul is warned by James and the elders that he is gaining a reputation for teaching all the Jews living among the Gentiles to disregard the law of Moses and not to circumcise their boys. So Paul follows the purification ritual in order to give the Jews no grounds to bring accusations against him for not following the Law. Paul causes a stir when he appears at the Temple because of his reputation. He escapes being killed by the crowd by allowing himself to be taken into Roman custody. When a plot to kill Paul on his way to appear before Jewish authority is discovered, he is transported by night to Caesarea. He is held as a prisoner there for two years until a new governor reopens his case in A.D. 59. When the governor suggests that he be sent back to Jerusalem for further trial, Paul uses his right as a Roman citizen to appeal to Caesar in Rome.

On the way to Rome, Paul is shipwrecked on Malta.

- Why does the ship get into trouble (Acts 27:21-26)?
- What happens to the sailors (Acts 27:42-44)?
- What happens after Paul is safely ashore on Malta (Acts 28:1-10)?

Three months later, Paul and the sailors head to Rome. Paul spends another two years under house arrest. Read Acts 28:30-31.

This is the last we read of Paul. The Bible does not say how or when Paul dies. Christian tradition holds that Paul was beheaded in Rome during the reign of Nero, around the mid-60s.

CONSIDER THE MARKS OF DISCIPLESHIP (10 MINUTES)

Disciples witness to others in order to lead them to Jesus Christ.

Have the group turn back to "Our Human Condition" in the Study Manual and read it aloud together.

Then have the group turn to the "Mark of Discipleship" printed in italics and read it aloud together.

1. As a group, discuss: Why do you think we tend to be hesitant to share our faith with others?

2. After reading and studying this session, how are you encouraged to be more willing to share with others?

3. In pairs, discuss the question in the "Marks of Discipleship" in your Study Manual that says, "Who are you? Think of ways you could use who you are and your experience to help lead people to Christ Jesus."

CLOSE WITH PRAYER (5 MINUTES)

Ask participants to turn to the next session in the Study Manual and write down their prayer requests.

Suggest we all continue to pray for the three people we thought of last week when we were challenged to "think of three people the Holy Spirit may be urging us to begin to pray for and invite into Christian fellowship." Consider inviting one of these persons to church this week. Pray for all three.

Close the group session in prayer.

6 THE GOSPEL PENETRATES THE WORLD

SMALL GROUP DISCUSSION GUIDE
(40 MINUTES TOTAL)

You have read many powerful events in the second half of Acts. Discuss the events listed below. Use your study notes and Bibles to help you. Look up the Scriptures when necessary.

Assign someone in your small group as timekeeper to ensure you spend at most 7–8 minutes per event.

Paul's Second Missionary Journey (Acts 15:36–18:28) (30 MINUTES)

1. Paul and Barnabas split. Paul takes Silas and heads toward Derbe and Lystra and then adds Timothy to his traveling group. Next, Paul has a vision of a man of Macedonia calling to him for help (Acts 15:36–16:10).

   - What is the vision (Acts 16:6-10)?

   - What does Paul do after the vision?

   - Paul had not intended to go to Europe but was persuaded in his dream.

   - Share with one another times you felt God was calling you in a different direction than you intended. What did you do? What happened?

2. Lydia is converted in Philippi (Acts 16:11-15).

   - Thinking about Jewish law and worship practices, as well as cultural practices and the role of women, what does this story tell us both about Lydia and Paul? about the gospel message?

3. In Philippi, Paul and Silas are stripped, beaten, and jailed when they cast out a spirit from a fortune-telling slave (Acts 16:16-24).

   - Why does casting out the spirit from the woman cause them to be jailed?

   - What happens in the night while they are in prison?

   - What is the result for the jailer and his family?

   - Share examples of times someone has converted to following Jesus because they have witnessed a miracle.

4. Athens is a city full of idols. Paul preaches in the synagogue. Paul debates with two groups, the Epicureans and the Stoics. They take him to a meeting of the Areopagus (council on religion and morals).

- Read Acts 17:22-23. Paul is finding common ground with his audience to begin his discussion about Christ. He continues when he quotes two Greek poets. When reading this part of Acts, we see how Paul is able to communicate with very educated people, find a common thought, and springboard into talking about Jesus.

- Share with one another examples of when you have been able to find common ground with someone and it opened the door for sharing faith.

Paul's Third Missionary Journey (Acts 18:23–21:17) (10 MINUTES)

5. Paul travels to Ephesus (Acts 19).

- If possible, have someone do an Internet search for *Ephesus Theatre*. Look at the picture. Notice the size of it. It could hold twenty-five thousand spectators.

- Also, do an Internet search for *Artemis of Ephesus*. Look at the picture of her, the goddess of fertility.

- What happens to cause the riot in Ephesus (Acts 19:23-41)?

7 PUT RIGHT WITH GOD THROUGH FAITH

PREPARE FOR THE SESSION

Make enough copies of the Small Group Discussion Guide (page 85) to distribute to groups of 4–6 people in your class.

WELCOME AND INTRODUCTION (5 MINUTES)

Greet participants and ask: How did you do with your daily reading this week?

Ask participants to open their Study Manuals to Session 7. Direct the group to read aloud together the following:

Theme Word: Justified

Theme Verse: "Therefore, since we are justified by faith, we have peace with God through our Lord Jesus Christ" (Romans 5:1, NRSV).

Title: Put Right With God Through Faith

Our Human Condition:

Part of the time we deliberately rebel. We do what we please. We go directly against God. But part of the time we "religious people" work hard to win God's approval, only to fail. We lack peace within ourselves and with others.

Ask participants to underline the parts of "Our Human Condition" they most easily understand.

Opening Prayer: Pray the prayer aloud together from this session in the Study Manual:

"Your loyal love, Lord, extends to the skies;
    your faithfulness reaches the clouds.
Your righteousness is like the strongest mountains;
    your justice is like the deepest sea" (Psalm 36:5-6).

VIEW THE DVD (5 MINUTES)

EXPLORE "PUT RIGHT WITH GOD THROUGH FAITH" (5 MINUTES)

Share the Following:

Look at a map of the Roman Empire in your Bible. This is often the last map in the back. Notice the distance from Jerusalem to Rome to Spain. In Paul's day, Rome controls all the land touching the Mediterranean Sea. There are an estimated forty-five million people living in this empire. Think about the city of Rome at the time of Paul. The population is 1.2 million; the Roman Forum and Circus Maximus exist, and the Coliseum is under construction.

The New Testament books begin with the four Gospels, then Acts, and then Letters, thirteen of which were attributed to the apostle Paul. Realize that the Letters are not in chronological order in the Bible. Instead, they are in order

7 PUT RIGHT WITH GOD THROUGH FAITH

of theological importance. The first one is the Letter to the Romans. It is a powerful statement of the Christian faith. The key concept is justification by faith.

ENCOURAGE SMALL GROUP DISCUSSION (20 MINUTES)

Divide the class into groups of 4–6. Hand out the Small Group Discussion Guide and ask the groups to spend the next twenty minutes on this activity.

Share the Following: (10 MINUTES)

In Romans many theological ideas and words are used. In your Study Manual you were asked to study Romans 3:21-26 and then rewrite the passage in your own words. In pairs, share with each other what you wrote. Then work together and rewrite this passage again, using both of your ideas. Spend about eight minutes.

Ask for a few volunteers to read their paraphrases to the whole class.

CONSIDER THE MARKS OF DISCIPLESHIP (25 MINUTES)

Disciples receive and trust the forgiving love of God in Jesus Christ and serve out of love and gratitude.

Have the group turn back to "Our Human Condition" in the Study Manual and read it aloud together. Then have the group turn to the "Mark of Discipleship" printed in italics and read it aloud together.

When we fully understand and experience justification through faith, we experience joy. We are free.

Freedom gives us lots of options in life, especially in our choices to serve. When we are not bound up by guilt, we can serve others out of a desire to share love and grace. Imagine doing things for others and giving time and money out of pure love for God.

Think a moment about this: When you choose to serve or help somebody, does your motivation ever come from the desire to earn God's approval, to earn others' approval, or to rid yourself of guilt and shame?

Turn to a person next to you and share some of the things that you do for others or for the church (for example, giving of your money or time). Then discuss what motivates you. Do you serve out of a sense of obligation or guilt or even shame? Or is it out of love and gratitude for what Christ has done for you?

In pairs, discuss as many of your responses in the "Marks of Discipleship" section as time allows.

CLOSE WITH PRAYER (5 MINUTES)

Ask participants to turn to the next session in the Study Manual and write down their prayer requests.

Close the group session with the following prayer:

Dear God, thank you that we are justified through faith. We no longer have any reason to try to work for our salvation. If in any areas of our lives we are feeling unforgiven, guilty, or bound up, help us to repent, turn that over to you, and accept your love and forgiveness. Lead us to places of service that enable us to share your love and grace with others. It is out of deep gratitude that we offer you this prayer. Amen.

SMALL GROUP DISCUSSION GUIDE

(20 MINUTES)

Discuss the following:

1. What is the difference between "atonement" in the Old Testament and "justification by faith" in the New Testament?

2. Consider the Jews at the time of Paul. For twelve hundred years, everything centers on following the Law and atoning for sins through animal and grain sacrifice at the Temple. When Paul writes, "We are justified by faith . . . through our Lord Jesus Christ," how might this theological understanding have challenged Jews? What about Gentiles?

3. Often a law clearly states what the penalty is when you break it, like the Old Testament law did. Sometimes clear penalty is easier to accept than justification by faith. Discuss why this is the case and give examples.

4. Understanding "justification by faith" can be difficult. However, in some situations, experiencing it can be even more difficult. For example, have you ever felt so unworthy of the forgiveness of your sin that you try to "pay for it yourself" rather than trusting that Christ's sacrifice is enough? In other words, have there been times you have felt so sinful that you are unable to accept and trust the forgiving power of God through Christ, and therefore you live in guilt and shame? Share examples with the group.

5. After reading Romans, what do you think Paul would say to you when you feel this way? Share your thoughts with the group.

6. What do you think helps people learn to trust God in all things, even in the ability to forgive all sins?

8 SOUND TEACHING FOR FAITHFUL LIVING

PREPARE FOR THE SESSION

Make enough copies of the Small Group Discussion Guide (page 89) to distribute to groups of 4–6 people in your class.

Be prepared to discuss with your group the possibility of extending your final session (Session 12) to two hours so that you may have a special celebration. Arrange a clergy to serve Communion. Preview Session 12 so you can plan ahead.

WELCOME AND INTRODUCTION (5 MINUTES)

Greet participants and ask: How did you do with your daily reading this week?

Ask participants to open their Study Manuals to Session 8. Direct the group to read aloud together the following:

Theme Word: Love

Theme Verse: "Pursue love, and use your ambition to try to get spiritual gifts" (1 Corinthians 14:1).

Title: Sound Teaching for Faithful Living

Our Human Condition:

We hate to leave the lifestyles of the secular world. They have a certain corrupt familiarity. But if we convert to the faith and fellowship of Christ, we discover that people, including ourselves, are still argumentative, divisive, self-centered. The church is not as perfect as we thought it would be.

Ask participants to underline the parts of "Our Human Condition" to which they most easily relate.

Opening Prayer: Pray the prayer aloud together from this session in the Study Manual:

> "Examine me, Lord; put me to the test!
>   Purify my mind and my heart.
> Because your faithful love is right in front of me—
>   I walk in your truth!" (Psalm 26:2-3).

VIEW THE DVD (5 MINUTES)

EXPLORE "SOUND TEACHING FOR FAITHFUL LIVING"
(10 MINUTES)

Share the Following:

The Corinthian church, full of new believers, is struggling and about to split because of a variety of issues causing disunity. Paul instructs them on how to deal with these problems. Paul urges all to be united in the same mind and the same purpose.

8 SOUND TEACHING FOR FAITHFUL LIVING

We see that Paul values every member of the body of Christ and believes all have spiritual gifts needed for a healthy church. Paul points out that there are specific gifts needed for those that are in church leadership. We see an example of church leaders Paul is nurturing when we look at Timothy and Titus, both young pastors. In the end, we will understand the importance of placing ourselves under sound teaching, using our spiritual gifts in the body of Christ, and living in love and unity.

ENCOURAGE SMALL GROUP DISCUSSION (30 MINUTES)

Divide the class into groups of 4–6. Hand out the Small Group Discussion Guide and ask the groups to spend the next thirty minutes on this activity.

LARGE GROUP DISCUSSION (10 MINUTES)

Remind everyone about the spiritual gifts inventory to be completed for Session 12. A reminder note is on the Small Group Discussion Guide and in the Study Manual.

Share the Following:

Discovering our spiritual gifts can help determine our role in the church and in life. Some people have the gifts of preaching, teaching, and leading in the church. We read about Timothy and Titus, two young pastors. Even as young pastors, they continually received sound teaching from their faithful leaders.

Their teaching included that they were to:
- Help people adhere to the central doctrines of the faith; concentrate on the essentials.
- Teach diligently. Teaching sound doctrine to growing Christians is a difficult and awesome responsibility.
- Respect spiritual authority and leadership.
- Teach the church to care for the needy.
- Be careful with money.

In discussing money, in 1 Timothy 6:10 we read, "The love of money is the root of all kinds of evil. Some have wandered away from the faith and have impaled themselves with a lot of pain because they made money their goal." Think carefully about this verse. How can we avoid "love of money"?

God still gifts and calls people to church leadership, some as teachers and even preachers. Have you ever considered a call to church leadership? Even as a preacher or teacher? Some here may feel called to ordained ministry. Some may be called to lead classes like this one. As we move toward our last session, prayerfully consider these thoughts.

CONSIDER THE MARKS OF DISCIPLESHIP (5 MINUTES)

Disciples seek sound teaching from faithful leaders and live in love.

Have the group turn back to "Our Human Condition" in the Study Manual and read it aloud together. Then have the group turn to the "Mark of Discipleship" printed in italics and read it aloud together.

As time allows, divide the group into groups of three or four to discuss the questions in the Study Manual under "Marks of Discipleship."

CLOSE WITH PRAYER (10 MINUTES)

Ask participants to turn to the next session in the Study Manual and write down their prayer requests.

Close the group session, praying aloud 1 Corinthians 13, thinking about your church. Remind participants that it was originally written to the church in Corinth.

SMALL GROUP DISCUSSION GUIDE
(30 MINUTES TOTAL)

There were several concerns affecting the unity of the Corinthian church. Here are some of the issues to discuss. Refer to your daily notes and the Study Manual to help with your discussion.

Sexual Conduct (1 Corinthians 5 and 6:12-20) (5 MINUTES)

1. What is the problem in the Corinthian church and what does Paul tell them to do?

The Role of Women in Church (1 Corinthians 14:33-35) (5 MINUTES)

2. What is the problem in the Corinthian church and what does Paul tell them to do?

Sound Teaching and Paul (10 MINUTES)

When we consider all Paul's advice to the Corinthian church, it can seem harsh and judgmental to us today. On the other hand, churches can err on the other extreme, where there seem to be no standards and "anything goes."

3. How do you think the church today can find truth in Paul's teachings and, at the same time, model unity, love, and grace?

Spiritual Gifts (10 MINUTES)

Several times in the New Testament the concept of spiritual gifts is mentioned. Spiritual gifts are roles or special abilities one receives through the Holy Spirit. The Holy Spirit distributes these gifts differently to each disciple. To learn a few of the gifts, read aloud 1 Corinthians 12:4-11.

In the rest of 1 Corinthians 12, Paul compares the spiritual gifts to the human body. There are different gifts, but they are all important to the body of Christ.

4. How do these gifts all work together for the common good?

5. How is the advice Paul gives to the Corinthians also useful to us?

To help you discover your spiritual gifts and ways your uniqueness can serve to strengthen the whole body of believers, you will begin working on your Spiritual Gifts Assignment at home this week. Go to *adultbiblestudies.com/fasttrack* to take the spiritual gifts inventory, and then turn to page 108 in the Study Manual for instructions on completing the Spiritual Gifts Assignment. We will spend most of our last session talking about your findings. Please have your assignment completed for the last session.

9 THE SON SHALL SET US FREE

PREPARE FOR THE SESSION

Make enough copies of the Small Group Discussion Guide (pages 92–93) to distribute to groups of 4–6 people in your class.

Be prepared to discuss with your group the possibility of extending your final session (Session 12) to two hours so that you may have a special celebration. Arrange for a clergy to serve Communion.

WELCOME AND INTRODUCTION (5 MINUTES)

Greet participants and ask: How did you do with your daily reading this week?

Ask participants to open their Study Manuals to Session 9. Direct the group to read aloud together the following:

Theme Word: Freedom

Theme Verse: "Christ has set us free for freedom. Therefore, stand firm and don't submit to the bondage of slavery again" (Galatians 5:1).

Title: The Son Shall Set Us Free

Our Human Condition:

I don't know if I'm free. There are so many rules. Sometimes I do my own thing, acting as if there were no moral restraints. But other times I try to be "religious" and follow the rules taught to me by my family or my church. When I try to follow all the rules, I fail and feel guilty. When I have some success, I feel religious; but I'm not very happy.

Ask participants to underline the parts of "Our Human Condition" to which they most easily relate.

Opening Prayer: Pray the prayer aloud together from this session in the Study Manual:

"Have mercy on me, God, according to your faithful love!
Wipe away my wrongdoings according to your great compassion!
Wash me completely clean of my guilt;
purify me from my sin!" (Psalm 51:1-2).

VIEW THE DVD (5 MINUTES)

EXPLORE "THE SON SHALL SET US FREE" (10 MINUTES)

Share the Following:

Paul's Letter to the Galatians is pivotal because it explains the fundamental difference between living by the Law and living by faith. Galatians helps us become free from a religion of rules without becoming morally reckless. We must avoid being "legalistic" on one hand or "libertine" on the other.

9 THE SON SHALL SET US FREE

As we begin our discussion of Galatians, let's briefly review the following topics and how they fit into Paul's teachings about living by the Law versus living by the Spirit. (Read Scriptures only if needed for additional information.)

- Jerusalem Council (Acts 15)

- Justification by faith alone (Galatians 2:16)

- Law of Moses (Galatians 3:2-3)

- Circumcision (Galatians 5:11-12)

Why was having freedom an important issue for the Galatian church?

Now, read aloud Galatians 5:13-15. What did being responsible with their freedom mean for the people in the Galatian church?

ENCOURAGE SMALL GROUP DISCUSSION (40 MINUTES)

Divide the class into groups of 4–6. Hand out the Small Group Discussion Guide and ask the groups to spend the next forty minutes on this activity.

CONSIDER THE MARKS OF DISCIPLESHIP (5 MINUTES)

Disciples experience and express freedom as loving God and loving neighbor.

Have the group turn back to "Our Human Condition" in the Study Manual and read it aloud together. Then have the group turn to the "Mark of Discipleship" printed in italics and read it aloud together.

CLOSE WITH PRAYER (10 MINUTES)

Ask participants to turn to the next session in the Study Manual and write down their prayer requests.
Close the group session with prayer.

9 THE SON SHALL SET US FREE

SMALL GROUP DISCUSSION GUIDE
(40 MINUTES TOTAL)

As we continue looking at the Book of Galatians, the overarching theme is living by the Law versus living by the Spirit.

The Freedom Lifestyle (15 MINUTES)

Read aloud Galatians 5:13-18. Believers are not only saved *by* Christ; they are called to live *in* Christ. The new life is the life of love.

1. What does it mean to live in Christ? How does this apply to your life?

As a new creation in Christ, we are to live *above* the Law and not *by* the Law. As Christians, we are to be led by the Holy Spirit. We are not tied to living by the Old Testament law. And yet, we can find ourselves in a trap of trying to live by a set of religious rules.

2. What examples can you think of where religious rules become more important than living in Christ? How have you gained freedom from these rules?

Read aloud Galatians 2:11-13. (Remember, Cephas is Peter.)

3. Like Peter, when have you been in a situation where peer pressure, or perhaps fatigue, caused you to revert back to a behavior prior to your life in Christ?

Living by the Flesh Versus Living by the Spirit (15 MINUTES)

4. If we are free from the Law, what keeps us from having no standards or boundaries— an "anything goes" lifestyle?

Read aloud Galatians 5:16-18 to your small group.

Have another person read aloud Galatians 5:19-21 (results of living by the flesh).

Have another person read aloud Galatians 5:22-25 (results of living by the Spirit).

As a group, compare and contrast the two ways of living.

5. What are the consequences of each?

6. How do you personally experience conflict between the desires of the flesh and the desires of the Spirit?

7. What are steps Christians can take to live by the power and the promptings of the Holy Spirit to conquer desires of the flesh?

THE SON SHALL
SET US FREE

Cheap Grace (10 MINUTES)

One of the problems in Christianity today is the idea that God is so loving and forgiving, that we have little to no responsibility as a Christian. In our Study Manual we read that Bonhoeffer said, "Cheap grace is . . . forgiveness without requiring repentance, . . . Communion without confession, . . . grace without discipleship, grace without the cross, grace without Jesus Christ."*

8. What is Bonhoeffer trying to say? What would it mean for you to move to a new costly grace without becoming legalistic?

Don't forget to take the spiritual gifts inventory at *adultbiblestudies.com/fasttrack* and work on the Spiritual Gifts Assignment on pages 108–109 of your Study Manual for review in Session 12.

* From Dietrich Bonhoeffer, *The Cost of Discipleship* (New York: The Macmillan Company, 1949), 35–36.

NOTES

PREPARE FOR THE SESSION

Make enough copies of the Small Group Discussion Guide (page 96) for Session 10 to distribute to groups of 4–6 people in your class.

Be prepared to discuss with your group the possibility of extending your final session (Session 12) to two hours so that you may have a special celebration. Arrange a clergy to serve Communion.

WELCOME AND INTRODUCTION (5 MINUTES)

Greet participants and ask: How did you do with your daily reading this week?

Ask participants to open their Study Manuals to Session 10. Direct the group to read aloud together the following:

Theme Word: Sacrifice

Theme Verses: "Also, let's hold on to the confession since we have a great high priest who passed through the heavens, who is Jesus, God's Son; because we don't have a high priest who can't sympathize with our weaknesses but instead one who was tempted in every way that we are, except without sin.

"Finally, let's draw near to the throne of favor with confidence so that we can receive mercy and find grace when we need help" (Hebrews 4:14-16).

Title: Our Great High Priest

Our Human Condition:

We cannot figure out a way to atone for our sins. Our faith grows weary and powerless. So we live lives of quiet desperation or turn to beating ourselves, wringing our hands, anesthetizing our spiritual pain with alcohol or other drugs, or developing neurotic symptoms.

Ask participants to underline the parts of "Our Human Condition" to which they most easily relate.

Opening Prayer: Pray the prayer aloud together from this session in the Study Manual:

> "You are LORD God All-Powerful!
>   No one is as loving
>   and faithful as you are" (Psalm 89:8, CEV).

VIEW THE DVD (5 MINUTES)

EXPLORE "OUR GREAT HIGH PRIEST" (10 MINUTES)

Share the Following:

Let's begin by quickly reviewing some key information we learned in the Old Testament about the sacrificial system that provided the way for the Hebrew people to atone for their sins. Have everyone refer to the Study Manual for assistance in answering these questions. Ask the following questions, using the answers in parentheses if needed for clarification.

• What was the process in the Old Testament for the purification of sins?

(Remember: Purification of sins [or, we would say, forgiveness] was through water [specific washing rituals], blood [specific animal sacrifices], and sacrifice [animal and grain offerings]. The sacrifice was prescribed and to be followed exactly to allow the person to be clean from moral, physical, and ritualistic impurity. Purification of sins involved the priest [as the mediator between the person and God].)

• What does the word *sanctify* mean?

(Remember: The process of becoming holy—to be set apart for God's service; to make fit for God's presence through cleansing from sin.)

• Who was the high priest?

(Remember: The high priest was the only priest who entered the Holy of Holies in the Tabernacle on the annual Day of Atonement [Yom Kippur]. He was required to do many purification washings and rituals and to wear a special robe on this day. He followed very specific rituals and prayers. He was the mediator between the people and God.)

• What is the new covenant? First, let me read aloud Hebrews 8:8-13.

(Remember: It is the new arrangement between God and God's people.)

Now, in our small groups, let's discuss further how Christ is the ultimate sacrifice.

ENCOURAGE SMALL GROUP DISCUSSION (35 MINUTES)

Divide the class into groups of 4–6. Hand out the Small Group Discussion Guide and ask the groups to spend the next thirty-five minutes on this activity.

CONSIDER THE MARKS OF DISCIPLESHIP (10 MINUTES)

Disciples accept God's forgiveness.

Have the group turn back to "Our Human Condition" in the Study Manual and read it aloud together. Then have the group turn to the "Mark of Discipleship" printed in italics and read it aloud together.

In pairs, discuss as many of the questions in the "Marks of Discipleship" section as you have time for.

CLOSE WITH PRAYER (10 MINUTES)

Ask participants to turn to the next session in the Study Manual and write down their prayer requests.

Close the group session by praying Hebrews 12:1-3.

SMALL GROUP DISCUSSION GUIDE
(35 MINUTES TOTAL)

Explore how Jesus becomes the mediator, the great High Priest, the ultimate sacrifice, and brings us into right relationship with God by discussing the following:

Jesus as the Final Sacrifice (15 MINUTES)

1. How do you understand Jesus Christ and his death on the cross as the final sacrifice for the forgiveness of sins in comparison to the sacrificial system in the Old Testament? (Refer to Hebrews 8:8-13 if needed.)

2. Read Hebrews 9:22 aloud. How do you understand the importance of Christ's blood shed on the cross in relationship to the forgiveness of sins?

3. Repentance is always a part of the sacrifice for forgiveness of sins. How serious do you take repentance when asking for forgiveness? Explain your answer.

4. Read Hebrews 10:26-27. As a person who accepts Jesus' sacrifice for the forgiveness of sins, what do you think are the consequences of deliberately sinning?

5. Read the third paragraph under the "Marks of Discipleship" that begins, "A pastor sometimes . . ." and discuss your response to the first question, "If that person could listen to you, what would you say?"

Jesus as the High Priest (10 MINUTES)

Read Hebrews 4:14-16.

Discuss the following questions:

1. What does this passage tell us about God?

2. What does this passage tell us about human beings?

3. What does this passage tell us about the relationship between God and people?

4. How do you feel about the idea that you can directly approach God through Jesus Christ, your High Priest?

Our Response to Christ's Sacrifice (10 MINUTES)

We have discussed Christ's sacrificial death on the cross for the forgiveness of our sins. In Hebrews 11, we read about all the people commended for their faith. They inspire us to hold firm to our faith in spite of our circumstances. They also inspire us to live a life of sacrifice ourselves.

Read Hebrews 13:15-16 aloud.

How do you live a sacrificial life? Allow time for each group member to share.

Don't forget to take the spiritual gifts inventory at *adultbiblestudies.com/fasttrack* and work on the Spiritual Gifts Assignment on pages 108–109 of your Study Manual for review in Session 12.

11 WE NEVER LOSE HOPE

PREPARE FOR THE SESSION

Make enough copies of the Small Group Discussion Guide (page 99) to distribute to groups of 4–6 people in your class.

Discuss final plans for your last session. Confirm with a clergy who will serve Communion.

WELCOME AND INTRODUCTION (5 MINUTES)

Greet participants and ask: How did you do with your daily reading this week?

Ask participants to open their Study Manuals to Session 11. Direct the group to read aloud together the following:

Theme Word: Victory

Theme Verses: "Then he said to me, 'These words are trustworthy and true. The Lord, the God of the spirits of the prophets, sent his angel to show his servants what must soon take place.

" 'Look! I'm coming soon. Favored is the one who keeps the words of the prophecy contained in this scroll' " (Revelation 22:6-7).

Title: We Never Lose Hope

Our Human Condition:

Wars and rumors of wars continue. Prejudice, crime, disease, and drugs pervade the planet. Weeping and pain and death are constant. Justice eludes us. Where is the victory? Where is hope?

Ask participants to circle the word or words in "Our Human Condition" to which they most relate.

Opening Prayer: Pray the prayer aloud together from this session in the Study Manual:

"Praise the LORD, all you nations!
  Worship him, all you peoples!
Because God's faithful love toward us is strong,
  the LORD's faithfulness lasts forever!
Praise the LORD!" (Psalm 117).

VIEW THE DVD (5 MINUTES)

EXPLORE "WE NEVER LOSE HOPE" (10 MINUTES)

Share the Following:

John receives his revelation from an angel during worship (Revelation 1:1-3). The revelation is apocalyptic, meaning "unveiling." Exactly what is being unveiled, and when and how it is going to happen, has been debated since this book was written; however, here is a basic overview of the Book of Revelation:

- In the beginning of Revelation, John is instructed to write down a message that Jesus is giving to each of the seven churches in Asia Minor (Revelation 1–3). The following chapters of Revelation are filled with symbolism and code words.

- The writer, John, is ushered to heaven to see what "must take place" (Revelation 4:1). John sees God holding a scroll secured with seven seals that only one person is worthy of breaking, someone described as "a Lamb, standing as if it had been slain" (Revelation 5:6).
- The Lamb, Jesus, begins to open the scroll. As Jesus breaks each of the seven seals on the scroll, John sees future disasters: war, famine, disease, Christians martyred, a massive earthquake, and, finally, falling stars crashing into Earth, forcing people to hide in caves.
- The vision continues with the seven trumpets, beasts, seven bowls, the destruction of Babylon, the coming of the New Jerusalem, Eden restored, and more.
- Then, near the end of his vision, John sees the martyred people of God gathered in heaven. He sees Satan and his followers thrown into a lake of fire. God's home becomes the dwelling place of everyone who has loved God. This dwelling place is where "there will be no mourning, crying, or pain" (Revelation 21:4).

Discuss: We know that John's revelation occurred when Christians were facing horrible persecution. Where in today's world do we see Christians experiencing persecution? How does this vision encourage disciples to remain faithful even in the midst of suffering?

Even though in this class we only briefly study Revelation, with its code words and difficult symbolism, the main point of the book is clear: In the end, God and goodness win; Satan and evil lose. People who love God will live with God forever.

The Bible has come full circle. Sin and death, which came as a result of disobedience in the garden of Eden, are destroyed.

John is overwhelmed with the victory at the end of his vision and closes with, "Come, Lord Jesus!" (Revelation 22:20).

ENCOURAGE SMALL GROUP DISCUSSION (35 MINUTES)

Divide the class into groups of 4–6. Hand out the Small Group Discussion Guide and ask the groups to spend the next thirty-five minutes on this activity.

CONSIDER THE MARKS OF DISCIPLESHIP (10 MINUTES)

Disciples remain faithful to God in the midst of persecution and suffering.

Have the group turn back to "Our Human Condition" in the Study Manual and read it aloud together. Then have the group turn to the "Mark of Discipleship" printed in italics and read it aloud together.

Discuss your answers to the questions under the "Marks of Discipleship" section in your Study Manual.

CLOSE WITH PRAYER (10 MINUTES)

Ask participants to turn to the next session in the Study Manual and write down their prayer requests.

Close the group session with prayer, thanking God and praying for the individuals mentioned in the final "Marks of Discipleship" question.

11 WE NEVER LOSE HOPE

SMALL GROUP DISCUSSION GUIDE
(35 MINUTES)

In Revelation 2–3, Jesus gives specific instructions to each of the seven churches in Asia Minor. In your small group, answer the following questions about each church. Use your homework notes and the Bible when needed. Spend 3–4 minutes on each church.

1. What does Jesus say about the church?

2. What does Jesus ask the churches to do in response to their situations?

   • Church in Ephesus (Revelation 2:1-7)

   • Church in Smyrna (Revelation 2:8-11)

   • Church in Pergamum (Revelation 2:12-17)

   • Church in Thyatira (Revelation 2:18-29)

   • Church in Sardis (Revelation 3:1-6)

   • Church in Philadelphia (Revelation 3:7-13)

   • Church in Laodicea (Revelation 3:14-22)

After completing your discussion of each of the churches, have each person in your group share his or her response to the following questions:

3. Which one of the seven churches do you identify with the most? Why?

4. What do you think you need to do in response?

Don't forget to take the spiritual gifts inventory at *adultbiblestudies.com/fasttrack* and work on the Spiritual Gifts Assignment on pages 108–109 of your Study Manual for review in Session 12.

If you make my word your home you will indeed be my disciples.
—John 8:31, NJB

12 A PEOPLE SET APART

PREPARE FOR THE SESSION

For the "sharing of spiritual gifts" part of this session, you need to plan the number of small groups you will have, based on allowing each person about seven minutes to share and whether you are extending this session to a two-hour time slot. If you are extending your session, you have sixty minutes for this part of the session that allows for sharing groups of 8–10 people. If you are not extending, divide your large group into small groups of 3–4 people. They will have twenty minutes to share. Each person shares for seven minutes.

Make enough copies of the Spiritual Gifts Discussion Guide (pages 103–104) to distribute to each of the small groups you have determined you will have for this part of your session. Each group will need to record the answers on the sheet turn in to the leader. Make sure you collect page 104 from each group at the end of the session so you will be able to help participants find their places of service.

Confirm Communion arrangements and your plan for closing worship with a clergy member. There is a suggested order of worship on page 105. You may want to include additional Scripture, liturgy, songs, prayers, and special music if you have extended time. Hopefully you will be able to celebrate Communion. Worship is planned to last twenty minutes.

WELCOME AND INTRODUCTION (5 MINUTES)

Greet participants and ask: How did you do with your daily reading this week?

Ask participants to open their Study Manuals to Session 12. Direct the group to read aloud together the following:

Theme Word: Ministry

Theme Verses: "We have many parts in one body, but the parts don't all have the same function. In the same way, though there are many of us, we are one body in Christ, and individually we belong to each other. We have different gifts that are consistent with God's grace that has been given to us" (Romans 12:4-6).

Title: A People Set Apart

Our Human Condition:

I don't like to be different. People ridicule others who seem strange and out of step with the crowd. And I surely don't want to be thought of as holy. But when I do try to serve God, sometimes I think that others can do so many things better than I can. I don't have any real talent or gifts that I can use in God's work.

Ask participants to circle the word or words in "Our Human Condition" to which they most relate.

Opening Prayer: Pray the prayer aloud together from this session in the Study Manual:

> "Teach me, Lord, what you want me to do,
> and I will obey you faithfully;
> teach me to serve you with complete devotion"
> (Psalm 86:11, GNT).

VIEW THE DVD (5 MINUTES)

EXPLORE "A PEOPLE SET APART" (15 MINUTES)

In today's session we are discussing what it means to be a holy people set apart for God. We will talk about what it means to be set apart in all our thoughts and actions.

Share the Following:

Read 1 Peter 2:9. What does this verse mean?

We are a set-apart, holy people. Holy people have an inner mark of character and an outer mark of compassion. Some things we must say no to. Some things we must say yes to.

Turn to a neighbor and discuss the following question: As a result of taking this study and of your commitment to Christ, what are some things in this world to which you need to say no? What are some things to which you need to say yes?

Share the Following:

We are all called to use our God-given gifts to serve. A few weeks ago, you were given a Spiritual Gifts Assignment. Hopefully, in the process of completing your homework, you came to appreciate that each of us is uniquely gifted to serve God. The homework activity was intended to help you understand your gifts so that you can and will find a place to serve that is meaningful to you.

SPIRITUAL GIFTS DISCUSSION (60 MINUTES for a 2-hour session, or 20 MINUTES if using a 75-minute session)

Each person will need about seven minutes to share. Divide your group into smaller groupings so that all will have their seven minutes of time in the time allotment you have chosen. Make sure you save thirty minutes at the end of this section for the closing.

Hand out the Spiritual Gifts Discussion Guide to each small group to spend the next sixty minutes completing it (twenty minutes if using a seventy-five-minute session).

Ask each participant to locate their copy of the Spiritual Gifts Assignment (Study Manual, pages 108–109).

When all are finished, collect the copies and give them to the proper person in the church who will follow up to get each person placed in their desired area of service and/or to discuss options.

CONSIDER THE MARKS OF DISCIPLESHIP (5 MINUTES)

Disciples know themselves as distinctive, peculiar people bearing the inner mark of character and the outer mark of compassion, committing their lives completely to God and using their gifts as ministry.

Have the group turn back to "Our Human Condition" in the Study Manual and read it aloud together. Then have the group turn to the "Mark of Discipleship" printed in italics and read it aloud together.

CLOSING WORSHIP (20 MINUTES)

Lead the closing worship you have planned, including serving Communion.

CLOSING (5 MINUTES)

Close the session and the class by

- thanking class members for their participation.
- encouraging class members to take action on their ideas for using their gifts to serve.
- sharing information on future plans and classes.

SPIRITUAL GIFTS DISCUSSION GUIDE
(7 MINUTES FOR EACH PERSON)

Complete all the steps for one person before moving to the next person (seven minutes for each person). Make sure one person in your group is recording information as instructed on page 104.

1. Have the person read from their Spiritual Gifts Discovery Assignment page the content of the following sections:

   - My spiritual gifts are . . .

   - Places I'm interested in serving are . . .

2. As the person finishes reading, have group members do the following:

   Confirm that person's thoughts and share any additional ideas about that person that you had when you wrote in your Study Manual.

   Have each person in the group share words of affirmation for that person. This could include sharing positive images or words of thankfulness from experiences during your study together.

3. Give the person a moment to respond to the affirmations and share what was most helpful or meaningful about being in the group this year.

4. As the person's portion concludes, have one group member say a prayer of thankfulness for that person.

Continue this process until all have shared and been prayed for by the group.

12 A PEOPLE SET APART

Ask one person in your group to record the following information about each person in your group as it is shared. Be sure to list their name, top 2–3 gifts, and the 1–3 places they are interested in serving. At the end of your group time, you will hand this sheet to your leader. Your leader will help the appropriate person(s) in your church/community know of your interests.

Name   **Gift or Gifts**   **Place or Intention of Service**

CLOSING WORSHIP

(20 MINUTES)

Read aloud the following:

We will close our Disciple FAST TRACK study by remembering we are a covenant people; by eating the meal of grace, Communion; and by committing our lives to Christian work and witness.

Covenant

By now we all know that we walk by faith, not alone but within a covenant community. In the beginning God called Abraham and Sarah to bring blessing to the world. The covenant had signs: land, descendants, circumcision, and Sabbath. Later, with Moses, the covenant meant deliverance, law, and liturgy. Always the covenant meant promise and hope.

Jesus Christ, the mediator of a new covenant, has put us right with God and has offered the sacrifice once and for all. Now as a covenant people we live in promise: Hebrews 13:14 reminds us,

"We don't have a permanent city here, but rather we are looking for the city that is still to come."

That city is the New Jerusalem, where God and the covenant people will dwell together.

Communion

Holy Communion is the common meal the covenant people eat together, remembering and waiting. Communion is a meal of grace. We come as we are. We are the least, the last, and the lost. God provides the food and all that it means. All we do is eat in faith, believing. We are sorry for our sins, eager to be changed, and hopeful of God's future. The meal is a sign and symbol of the covenant community.

(If you are able to have the sacrament of Holy Communion, have the clergy serve Communion here.)

Commitment

When Isaiah was called, he responded, "I'm here; send me." So will we.

We know now from Scripture that to be God's people means to do God's work. We must be a people set apart. Jesus taught, "You are the salt of the earth" (Matthew 5:13). Our saltiness is what God is doing through us to save a lost world.

God was not satisfied only to restore Israel after captivity; God gave Israel a mission: Isaiah said,

"I will . . . appoint you as light to the nations
so that my salvation may reach to the end of the earth" (Isaiah 49:6).

Our Lord stood on the mountain and gave his post-Resurrection command to his disciples:

"Therefore, go and make disciples of all nations" (Matthew 28:19).

Closing Prayer

Gather hands in a circle and close your time together in prayer. Close with "Amen."

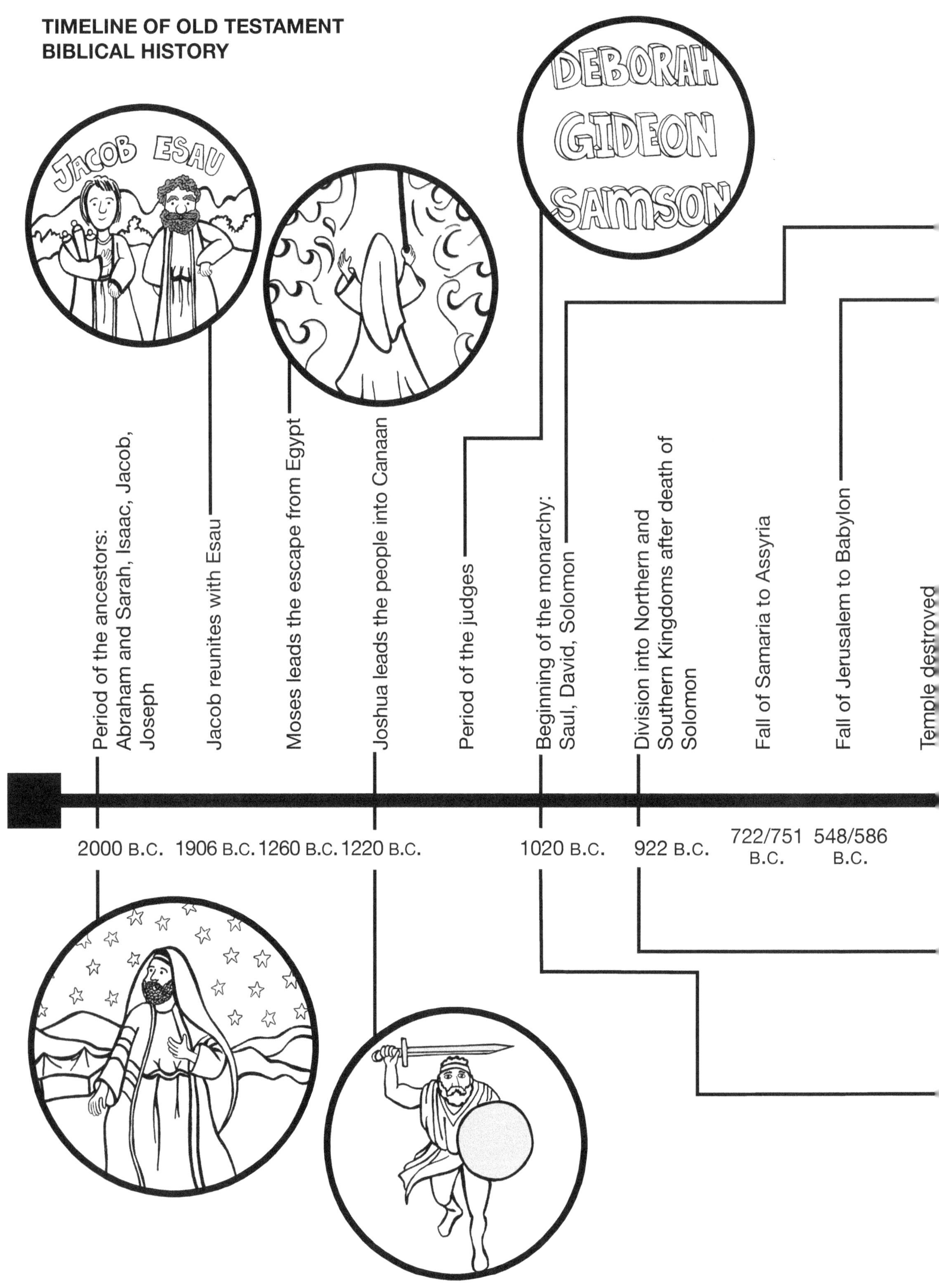

TIMELINE OF OLD TESTAMENT
BIBLICAL HISTORY

JACOB ESAU

DEBORAH
GIDEON
SAMSON

Period of the ancestors:
Abraham and Sarah, Isaac, Jacob,
Joseph

Jacob reunites with Esau

Moses leads the escape from Egypt

Joshua leads the people into Canaan

Period of the judges

Beginning of the monarchy:
Saul, David, Solomon

Division into Northern and
Southern Kingdoms after death of
Solomon

Fall of Samaria to Assyria

Fall of Jerusalem to Babylon

Temple destroyed

2000 B.C.   1906 B.C. 1260 B.C. 1220 B.C.   1020 B.C.   922 B.C.   722/751   548/586
                                                                          B.C.   B.C.

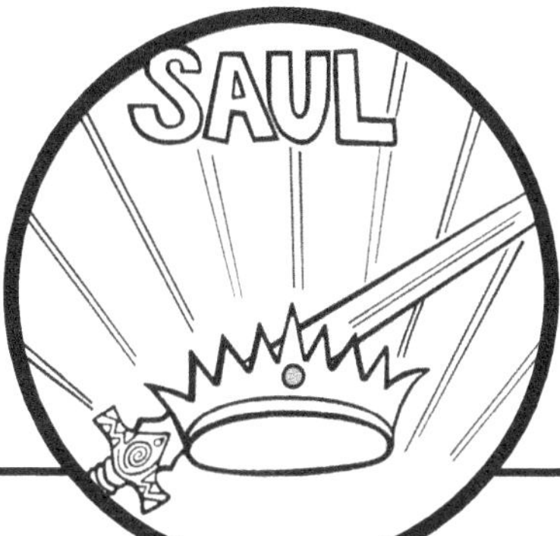

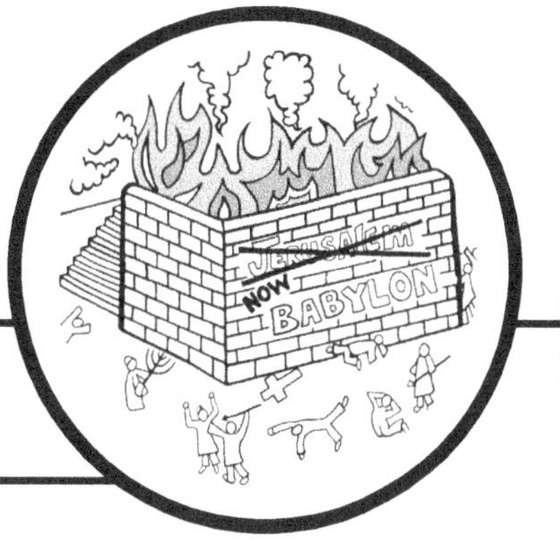

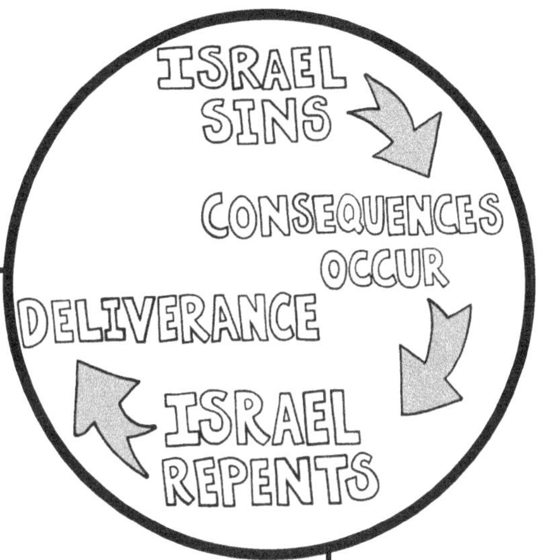

Persian Period

Edict of Cyrus

Return of exiles

Temple rebuilt

Greek Period

Alexander the Great

Jews revolt (Hasmonean Period)

Romans capture Jerusalem

Herod the Great appointed king over Palestine

Birth of Jesus

539 B.C. 538 B.C. 515 B.C. 333 B.C. 167 B.C. 63 B.C. 37 B.C. 4 B.C.

To download and print this timeline, go to *adultbiblestudies.com/fasttrack*.

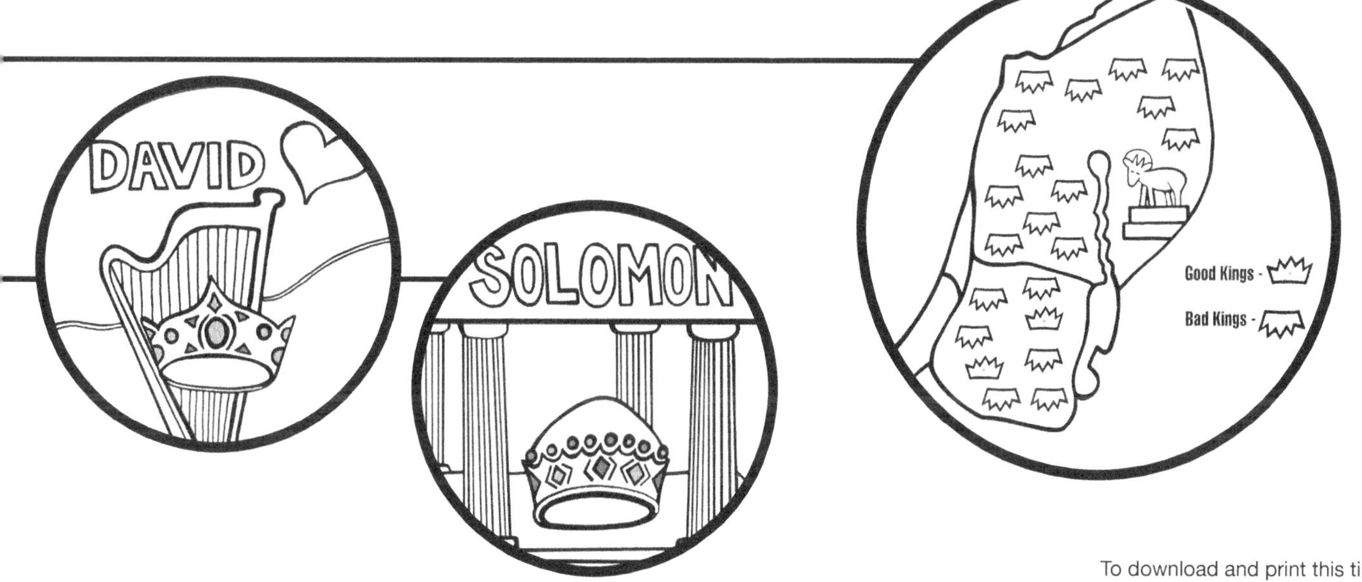

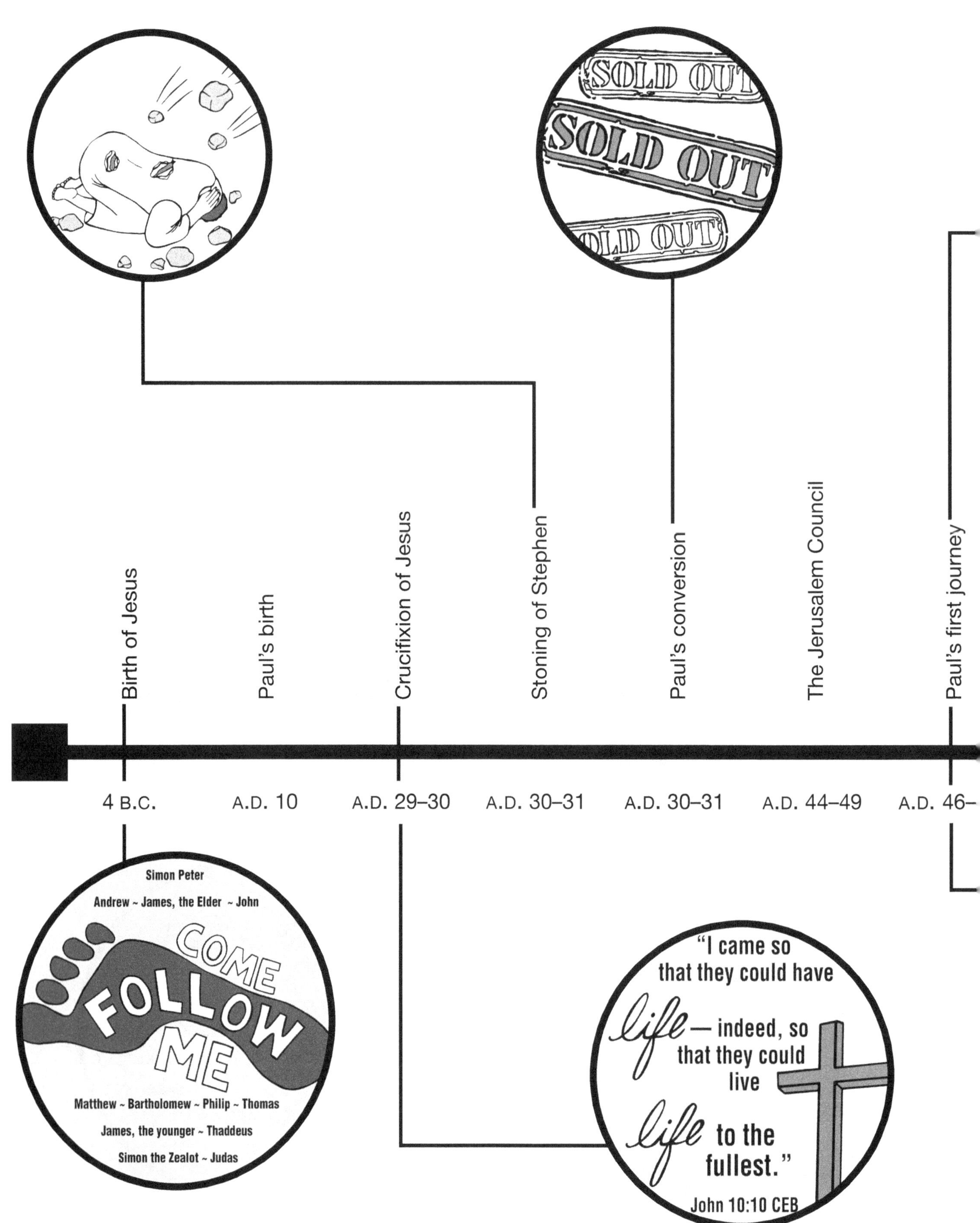

TIMELINE OF NEW TESTAMENT
BIBLICAL HISTORY

SOLD OUT
SOLD OUT
SOLD OUT

Birth of Jesus
Paul's birth
Crucifixion of Jesus
Stoning of Stephen
Paul's conversion
The Jerusalem Council
Paul's first journey

4 B.C.
A.D. 10
A.D. 29–30
A.D. 30–31
A.D. 30–31
A.D. 44–49
A.D. 46–

Simon Peter
Andrew ~ James, the Elder ~ John

COME
FOLLOW
ME

Matthew ~ Bartholomew ~ Philip ~ Thomas
James, the younger ~ Thaddeus
Simon the Zealot ~ Judas

"I came so
that they could have
life — indeed, so
that they could
live
life to the
fullest."
John 10:10 CEB

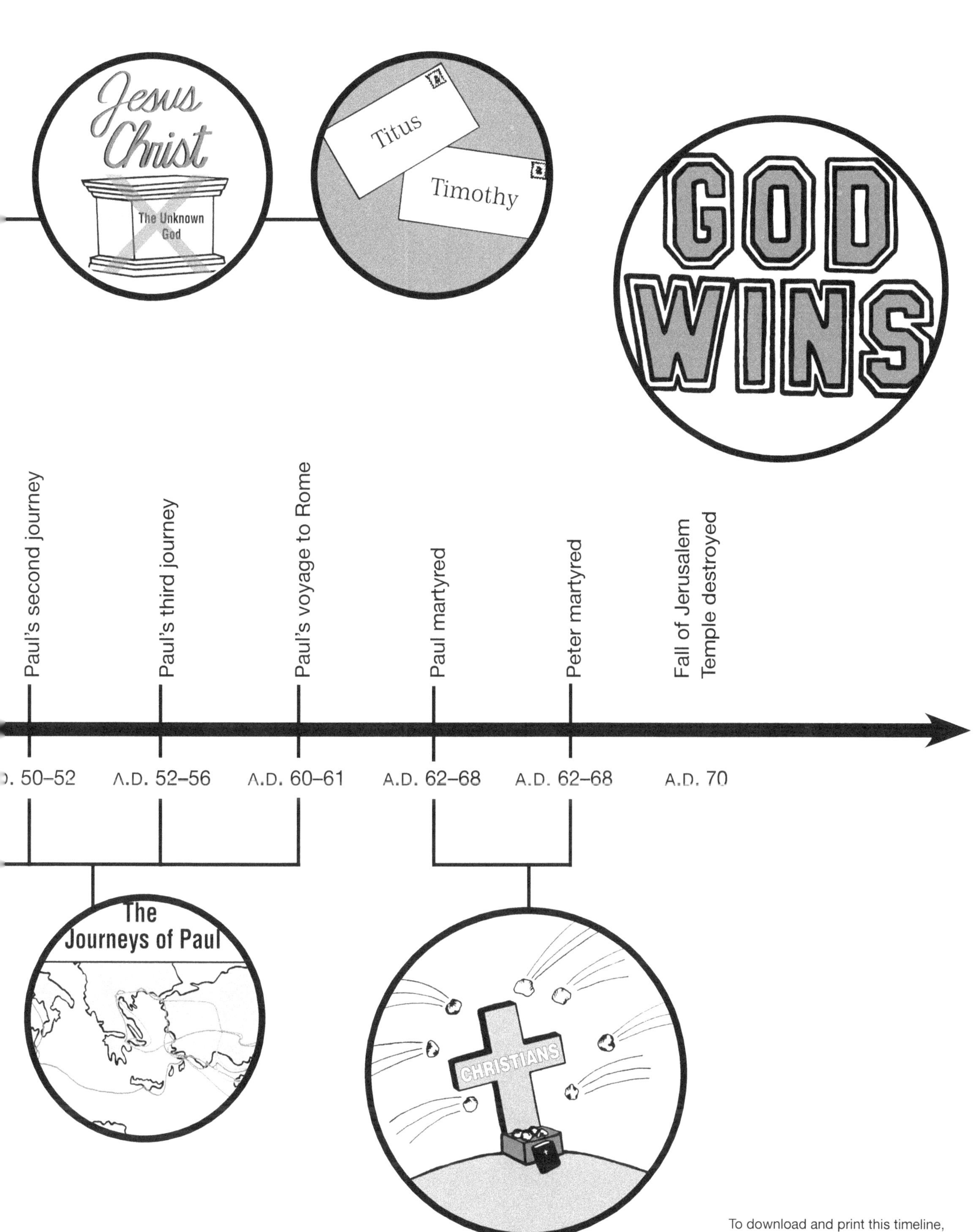

Jesus Christ
The Unknown God
Titus
Timothy
GOD WINS
Paul's second journey
Paul's third journey
Paul's voyage to Rome
Paul martyred
Peter martyred
Fall of Jerusalem Temple destroyed
A.D. 50–52
A.D. 52–56
A.D. 60–61
A.D. 62–68
A.D. 62–68
A.D. 70
The Journeys of Paul
CHRISTIANS